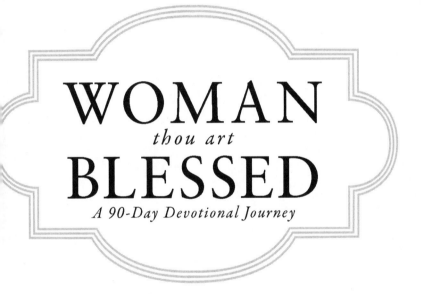

WOMAN

thou art

BLESSED

A 90-Day Devotional Journey

WOMAN
thou art
BLESSED
A 90-Day Devotional Journey

T.D. JAKES

DESTINY IMAGE® PUBLISHERS, INC.

P.O. Box 310, Shippensburg, PA 17257-0310

"Promoting Inspired Lives."

This book and all other Destiny Image and Destiny Image Fiction books are available at Christian bookstores and distributors worldwide.

Cover design by Eileen Rockwell
Interior design by Terry Clifton

For more information on foreign distributors, call 717-532-3040.

Reach us on the Internet: www.destinyimage.com.

ISBN 13 TP: 978-0-7684-5276-1
ISBN 13 eBook: 978-0-7684-5274-7
ISBN 13 HC: 978-0-7684-5273-0
ISBN 13 LP: 978-0-7684-5275-4

For Worldwide Distribution, Printed in the U.S.A.
1 2 3 4 5 6 7 8 / 25 24 23 22 21

CONTENTS

Introduction

To the beautiful woman of God who knows there is more, I am writing this for you. To the woman of God who feels heavy laden and weighed down by life's circumstances, I am writing this for you. To the woman who knows she is created to soar and shine for God, this is your time! God placed His divine purpose and prophetic promises in you at creation. They are still within you, ready to burst forth. If the past is still haunting you, fear not. If you feel like you're in the fire, fear not. There is a fourth Man in the fire, and He wants to set you free. When you belong to God, the fire only burns the ties that bind you. It might get hot, but God always provides a way of escape. You will come out shining like gold.

I pray that we as Christians never lose our conviction that God does change lives. We must protect this message. Our God enables us to make the radical changes necessary for fulfilling our purposes and responsibilities. Like the caterpillar that eats and sleeps its way into change, the process occurs gradually, but nonetheless powerfully. When we let God do this transformation work in our lives, we come out as beautiful butterflies, soaring with Him. Many people who will rock this world are sleeping in the cocoon of obscurity, waiting for their change to come. The Scriptures declare, *"...it is high time to awake out of sleep; for now our salvation is nearer than when we first believed."* (Rom. 13:11). Beloved, it's just your time!

Change is a gift from God. It is given to the woman who finds herself too far removed from what she feels destiny has ordained for her. There is nothing wrong with being wrong—but there is something wrong with not making the necessary adjustments to get things right! Even within the Christian community, some do not believe in God's ability to change the human heart. This unbelief in God's ability to change causes people to judge others on the basis of their past. Dead issues are periodically revived in the mouths of gossips. Still, the Lord progressively regenerates the mind of His children.

Don't assume that real change occurs without struggle and prayer. However, change can be achieved. Life has chiseled many of us into mere fragments of who we were meant to be. To all who receive Him, Christ gives the power to slip out of who they were forced into being so they can transform into the individual they each were created to be.

Daughter, God knows who you truly are and what He has prepared for you to do. He has blessings that are just for you. To fulfill your purpose and rock this world, you, just like that caterpillar, will need to go through a transformation journey with the Lord. This devotional journal will take you through a process of change and growth unto your specific purpose. It might feel like that dark cocoon on some days as we bury old mindsets and nail past traumas to the cross. There will be Gethsemane, "oil press" moments of crying out to the Lord as we deal with identity, relationships, and your ways of thinking. But it is through the fire that God makes us pure gold.

Don't rush your way through this journal. Change takes time. Each day has a Scripture, a devotional entry, a Purpose Point quote, and a Transformation Moment. Let the material really sink in as you read. Pray with me about each important topic and let God transform your heart. He surely will.

The cost to change includes prayers, tears, and struggle, but I assure you it will be well worth the effort. No matter what life has chiseled from you, God has the final word. You won't finish looking like you did at the start. He makes all things new. Remember, thou art blessed! Are you ready for transformation?

THE POWER TO TRANSFORM IS WITHIN YOU!

Before I formed you in the womb I knew
you; before you were born I sanctified you;
I ordained you a prophet to the nations.
JEREMIAH 1:5

God taught me an important lesson about transformation through my twin boys. Children are excellent teachers. They were playing with a truck, then the next time I looked it was an airplane. I asked, "What happened to the truck you were playing with?" They explained, "Daddy, this is a transformer!" I then inquired, "What is a transformer?" Their answer brought me into the Presence of the Lord. They said, "It can be transformed from what it was before into whatever we want it to be!"

Suddenly I realized that God had made the first transformer! He created man from dust. He created him in such a way that, if need be, He could pull a woman out of him without ever having to reach back into the dust. Out of one creative act God transformed the man into a marriage. Then He transformed the marriage into a family, the family into a society, etc. God never had to reach into the ground again because the power to transform was intrinsically placed into man (and woman!). All types of potential were locked into your spirit before birth. For the Christian, transformation at its optimum is the outworking of the internal. God placed certain things in you that must come out. Daughter, you house the prophetic power of God. Every word of your personal prophetic destiny is inside you. He has ordained you to be!

It is God who works out the internal destinies of men and women. He gives us the power to become who we are eternally and internally. What Christians so often refer to as grace truly is God's divine enablement to accomplish predestined purpose. When the Lord says to Paul, *"My grace is sufficient for you..."* (2 Cor. 12:9), He is simply stating that His power is not intimidated by your circumstances. It is important that each and every vessel God uses realize that they were able to accomplish what others could not only because God gave them the grace to do so. You are empowered by God to reach and accomplish goals that transcend human limitations!

PURPOSE POINT: You house the prophetic power of God. Every word of your personal prophetic destiny is inside you.

TRANSFORMATION MOMENT: Mighty woman of God, God placed a prophetic destiny inside of you. He has a great purpose for your life. If you are weary from trying to unlock our own resources, come to the Lord, receive Him, and allow Him to release in you the power to become whatever you need to be. He will show you your purpose afresh. God is the One who made you. He knows your potential. He also knows everything you've been through, and He's not worried. He is giving you the grace and power to become who you really are and fulfill your destiny.

As you embark on this journey, invite the Holy Spirit to awaken your spirit to His voice again. Ask God to remind you of your prophetic destiny. Who does He say you are? What has been hidden that He wants to release through this transformation process?

WOMAN *Thou Art* BLESSED

PURSUE GOD, THE ULTIMATE RABBI

So the Lord said to Moses: "Gather to Me seventy
men of the elders of Israel, whom you know
to be the elders of the people and officers over
them; bring them to the tabernacle of meeting,
that they may stand there with you."
NUMBERS 11:16

Today in the Body of Christ a great deal of emphasis is placed on the process of mentoring. The concept of mentoring is both scriptural and effective; however, as we often do, many of us have gone to extremes. Instead of teaching young people to pursue God, the ultimate Rabbi, they are running amuck looking for a spiritual mother or father to pour into them. All of us are not mentored as Joshua was—under the firm hand of a strong leader. Some, like Moses, are prepared by the workings of the manifold wisdom of God.

This latter group receive mentoring through the carefully orchestrated circumstances that God ordains to accomplish an end result. Regardless of which describes your ascent to greatness, it is still God who *"worketh in you both to will and to do."* When you understand this, you appreciate the people or the methods God used, but ultimately praise the God whose masterful ability to conduct has crescendoed in the finished product of a man or woman of God.

In keeping with this mentoring concept, let's consider Moses' instructions when asked to consecrate elders in Israel. God told Moses to gather unto Him men whom he knew were elders. God says, *"I want you to separate men to be elders who are elders."* You can only ordain someone to be what he or she already is. The insight we need to succeed is the discernment of who is among us. Woe unto the woman who is placed into what she is not. Moses was to bring these men into a full circle. In other words, they were to be led into what they already were. We are fulfilled only when we are led into being who we were predestined to be. Real success is coming to ourselves. Who are you, beloved?

PURPOSE POINT: We are fulfilled only when we are led into being who we were predestined to be. Real success is coming to ourselves.

TRANSFORMATION MOMENT: Maybe you have wonderful mentors or maybe you long for more mentorship. Regardless of who else is or is not pouring into you, God is working in your life. He is the One orchestrating circumstances and even people around you to accomplish His purposes because He knows your identity and purpose. He is leading you to real success: coming to yourself...your shining, beautiful self.

Even as we mentor others or seek to be mentored, it is important to remember what God showed Moses. He needed to discern the giftings and callings in these men and ordain them into who they were, in this case, elders. In your process of coming to yourself, pursue God, the ultimate Rabbi. He will show you more and more of what is in you!

REPENTANCE IS THE PREREQUISITE OF REVIVAL

God exalted him to his own right hand as
Prince and Savior that he might bring Israel
to repentance and forgive their sins.
ACTS 5:31 (NIV)

The Bible calls change *repentance*. Repentance is God's gift to a struggling heart who wants to find herself. The Lord wants to bring you to a place of safety and shelter. Without the Holy Spirit's help you can search and search and still not find repentance. The Lord will show the place of repentance only to those who hunger and thirst after righteousness. One moment with the Spirit of God can lead you into a place of renewal that, on your own, you would not find or enjoy. When God gives you the grace to make changes that you know you couldn't do with your own strength, it becomes precious to you.

> *For you know that afterward, when he wanted*
> *to inherit the blessing, he was rejected, for he*
> *found no place for repentance, though he sought*
> *it diligently with tears* (Hebrews 12:17).

Brother Esau sought for the place of repentance and could not secure it. To be transformed is to be changed. If you are not moving into your divine purpose, you desperately need to repent. "Repent" has a strong negative connotation for the person indoctrinated to believe that repentance is a fearful and dangerous action. It is not dangerous. Repentance is the prerequisite of revival. There cannot be revival without prayerful repentance. John the Baptist taught Israel, *"Repent ye: for the kingdom of heaven is at hand"* (Matt. 3:2). If God wants you to change, it is because He wants you to be prepared for what He desires to do next in your life. Get ready daughter; the best is yet to come.

✦ **PURPOSE POINT:** Repentance is the prerequisite of revival. There cannot be revival without prayerful repentance.

✦ **TRANSFORMATION MOMENT:** Many of us are crying out for revival to come in our nations, our cities, our families, and in our own hearts. But there cannot be revival without prayerful repentance. Repentance is not dangerous or negative. It is precious. God wants to prepare you and bring you out of that cocoon we started out with so you can fly in full color and beauty. You can't come out the same as you were when you went in. He wants you to become the stunning butterfly and fulfill your purposes as who you truly are.

As you seek for righteousness, the Holy Spirit will show you anything that needs His transforming touch. Ask Him to reveal any areas where you need to repent. And please don't let that word put you off. Simply follow Jesus into any change needed to align your heart with His divine purpose.

BE CONFORMED BY GETHSEMANE, NOT THE WORLD

For whom He foreknew, He also predestined to be conformed to the image of His Son, that He might be the firstborn among many brethren.
ROMANS 8:29

The word *conformed* in Romans 8:29 is *summorphoo* (James Strong, *The Exhaustive Concordance of the Bible* [Peabody, MA: Hendrickson Publishers, n.d.], #G4832), which means "to be fashioned like or shaped into the image or the picture" of—in this case—Christ. God has predestined you to shape up into a picture of Christ in the earth. Christ is the firstborn of a huge family of siblings who all bear a striking resemblance to their Father. The shaping of a will, however, requires a visit to the garden of Gethsemane. *Gethsemane* literally means "oil press" (Strong's #G1068). God presses the oil of His anointing out of your life through adversity. When you forsake your will in order to be shaped into a clearer picture of Christ, you will see little drops of oil coming out in your walk and work for God. In short, He predestined the pressing in your life that produces the oil. As you are pressed, you gradually conform to the image of your predestined purpose.

> *And do not be conformed to this world, but be transformed by the renewing of your mind, that you may prove what is that good and acceptable and perfect will of God.* (Romans 12:2).

Literally, this verse says we are not to be conformed to the same pattern of this world. The text warns us against submitting to the dictates of the world. We are to avoid using those standards as a pattern for our progress. On a deeper level God is saying, "Do not use the same pattern of the world to measure success or to establish character and values." The term *world* in Greek is *aion* (Strong's #G165), which refers to ages. Together these words tell us, "Do not allow the pattern of the times you are in to become the pattern that shapes your inward person."

🕊 **PURPOSE POINT:** Christ is the firstborn of a huge family of siblings who all bear a striking resemblance to their Father.

🕊 **TRANSFORMATION MOMENT:** God predestined you to be conformed to the image of Jesus, a beloved child of God. Jesus went to the garden of Gethsemane. He sweat drops of blood in fervent prayer before His Father, laying down His will for the Father's biggest plan of transformation for mankind. The standards of this world might say that adversity means you did something wrong, but God has a different standard. He uses adversity to press you and develop your character.

When you forsake your will for His ways, you will see little drops of oil coming out in your walk and work for God. He squeezes you right into your purpose if you let Him. Are there any areas of adversity in your life right now? Ask God to show you the oil coming from those very places.

DON'T BE CONFORMED, BE TRANSFORMED!

*You were taught, with regard to your former way of
life, to put off your old self, which is being corrupted
by its deceitful desires; to be made new in the attitude
of your minds; and to put on the new self, created
to be like God in true righteousness and holiness.*

EPHESIANS 4:22-24 (NIV)

A s we continue on this topic of not being conformed
to this world, some questions might come to mind:
"How do you respond to the preexisting circumstances and
conditions that have greatly affected you?" Or, "I am already
shaped into something less than what God would want me to
be because of the times in which I live or the circumstances
in which I grew up." The answer is this: every aspect of your
being that has already been conformed to this age must
be transformed!

The prefix *trans* implies movement, as in the words
transport, translate, transact, transition, etc. In this light,
transform would imply moving the form. On a deeper level
it means moving from one form into another, as in the tad-
pole that is transformed into the frog and the caterpillar into

the butterfly. No matter what has misfigured you, in God is the power to be transformed. He makes all things new (see Isa. 43:18-19).

Many individuals in the Body of Christ are persevering without progressing. They wrestle with areas that have been conformed to the world instead of transformed. Transformation takes place in the mind. The Bible teaches that we are to be renewed by the transforming of our minds (see Rom. 12:2; Eph. 4:23). Only the Holy Spirit knows how to renew the mind. The struggle we have inside us is with our self-perception. Generally our perception of ourselves is affected by those around us. Our early opinion of ourselves is deeply affected by the opinions of the authoritative figures in our formative years. If our parents tend to neglect or ignore us, it tears at our self-worth. Eventually, though, we mature to the degree where we can walk in the light of our own self-image, without it being diluted by the contributions of others.

PURPOSE POINT: No matter what has misfigured you, in God is the power to be transformed.

TRANSFORMATION MOMENT: All of us have been affected by past circumstances. Maybe you can still hear negative words ringing in your ears. Maybe your heart believed those words or past experiences and your self-perception is still suffering. Fear not, daughter! The Holy Spirit knows how to renew your mind. He wants to bring you to the place of maturity where your self-image comes directly from Him. You are a mighty woman of the Most High God!

What do you really believe about yourself? Does it line up with what Scripture says about your identity and worth? If not, it is time to be transformed by the renewing of your mind. A powerful place to start is by listing Scriptures about your value and identity (for example Psalm 139). Read them over yourself. Let the words sink in deep and drown out every other voice.

TRANSFORMING TRUTHS ARE BIRTHED IN HIS PRESENCE

He said to them, "But who do you say that I am?" Simon Peter answered and said, "You are the Christ, the Son of the living God."
MATTHEW 16:15-16

When we experience the new birth, we again go back to the formative years of being deeply impressionable. It's important to be discerning in who we allow to influence us. Whenever we become intimate with someone, the first thing we should want to know is, "Who do you say that I am?" Our basic need is to be understood by the inner circle of people with whom we walk. However, we must be ready to abort negative, destructive information that doesn't bring us into an accelerated awareness of inner realities and strengths. Jesus was able to ask Peter, *"Who do you say that I am?"* because He already knew the answer! (See Matthew 16:15.) Jesus knew who He was.

To ask someone to define you without first knowing the answer within yourself is dangerous. When we ask that kind of question, without an inner awareness, we open the door for manipulation. The Lord wants to help you realize who you are and what you are graced to do. When you understand that He is the only One who really knows you, then you pursue Him with fierceness and determination. Only God knows who we are and how we are to attain. This knowledge, locked up in the counsel of God's omniscience, is the basis of our pursuit, and it is the release of that knowledge that brings immediate transformation. He knows the hope or the goal of our calling. He is not far removed from us; He reveals Himself to people who seek Him. The finders are the seekers. The door is opened only to the knockers and the gifts are given to the askers! (See Luke 11:9.)

Transforming truths are brought forth through the birth canal of our diligence in seeking His face. Initiation is our responsibility. Whosoever hungers and thirsts shall be filled. It is while you are in His presence that He utters omniscient insights into your individual purpose and course. There is a renewing word that will change your mind about your circumstance. Just when the enemy thinks he has you, transform before his very eyes!

PURPOSE POINT: When you understand that He is the only One who really knows you, then you pursue Him with fierceness and determination.

TRANSFORMATION MOMENT: One of the most dangerous things in life is to lose track of who you are. Sometimes others see the hidden treasures within us, but other times they put false labels on us or define us based on our past. God wants to release the truth that brings transformation. This comes through time in His presence. As you seek Him, not only do you find Him, but you find the real you. Then, whenever someone tells you what you can't do or be, or what you can't get or attain, then tell them, "I can do all things through Christ who strengthens me! I am a transformer!"

Are there places where you've asked others to define you? Seek Jesus instead. Knock on Heaven's door today and ask God to open your eyes to see what He sees when He looks at you.

RISE UP AND WALK, MY FRIEND

When Jesus saw him lying there, and knew that he
already had been in that condition a long time, He
said to him, "Do you want to be made well?" ...Jesus
said to him, "Rise, take up your bed and walk."
JOHN 5:6 and 8

Jesus told a woman who had been wrestling with a crippling condition for 18 years that she was not really bound— that in fact she was loosed! Immediately she was transformed by the renewing of her mind. (See Luke 13:11-13.) Paul said in Ephesians 5:26 that Jesus cleanses by the *"washing of water by the word."* His profound truth washes away every limitation and residue of past obstacles and gradually, luxuriously, transforms us into the refreshed, renewed people we were created to become.

With one word, Jesus changes everything, but we have to respond. Jesus seldom attended funerals. When He did, it was to arrest death and stop the ceremony. If you are planning an elaborate ceremony to celebrate your nonparticipation in the plan of God, I must warn you that God doesn't hang around funerals. Sometimes Christians become frustrated and withdraw from activity on the basis of personal struggles. They think it's all over, but God says not so! The best is yet to come. The Lord doesn't like pity parties, and those who have them are shocked to find that although He is invited, He seldom attends. Many morbid mourners will come to sit with you as you weep over your dear departed dreams. But if you want the Lord to come, you mustn't tell Him that you are not planning to get up.

If we intend to accomplish anything, we must react to adversity like yeast. Once yeast is thoroughly stirred into the dough, it cannot be detected. Although it is invisible, it is highly effective. When the heat is on, it will rise. The warmer the circumstance, the greater the reaction. Likewise, God sets us in warm, uncomfortable places so we can rise. Consider Israel in Egypt. The more the enemy afflicted them, the more the Israelites grew. Sometimes the worst times in our lives do more to strengthen us than all our mountaintop experiences. The power of God reacts to struggle and stress. Isn't that what God meant when He told Paul, *"...My strength is made perfect in weakness..."* (2 Cor. 12:9).

🌿 PURPOSE POINT: Sometimes the worst times in our lives do more to strengthen us than all our mountaintop experiences.

🌿 TRANSFORMATION MOMENT: We all go through personal struggles. Sometimes God even sets us in uncomfortable places so we can rise and grow. Then, we have two choices: throw ourselves a pity party or get up and walk. Like the infirmed man in John 5, at times we don't feel strong enough to move at all, but Jesus meets us in our lowest places. His power actually increases when we feel weak. He extends supernatural healing and says, *"Rise, take up your bed, and walk!"* (John 5:8). Beloved, will you respond to His invitation?

Are you in a warm, uncomfortable place? If you feel the fire heating up around you, react to the adversity like yeast. Grab hold of Jesus's outstretched hand and let Him pull you up. Don't stay down. Rise up, daughter, the best is yet to come.

DON'T STAY IN THE BOAT...
WALK ON WATER!

So He said, "Come." And when Peter had come down
out of the boat, he walked on the water to go to Jesus.
But when he saw [a]that the wind was boisterous,
he was afraid; and beginning to sink he cried out,
saying, "Lord, save me!" And immediately Jesus
stretched out His hand and caught him, and said to
him, "O you of little faith, why did you doubt?"
MATTHEW 14:29-31

If you ever get around people who have accomplished much, they will tell you that those accomplishments didn't come without price. Generally that cost is much more expensive than you normally want to pay. Still, the cost of total transformation means different things to different people. When you arrive at your destination, don't be surprised that some people will assume everything you achieved came without price. The real price of success lies within the need to persevere. The trophy is never given to someone who does not complete the task. Setbacks are just setups for God to show what He is able to do. Funerals are for people who have accepted the thought that everything is over. Don't do that; instead tell the enemy, "I am not dead yet."

The whole theme of Christianity is one of rising again. However, you can't rise until you fall. Now that doesn't mean you should fall into sin. It means you should allow the resurrecting power of the Holy Spirit to operate in your life regardless of whether you have fallen into sin, discouragement, apathy, or fear. There are obstacles that can trip you as you escalate toward productivity. But it doesn't matter what tripped you; it matters that you rise up. People who never experience these things generally are people who don't do anything. There is a certain safety in being dormant. Nothing is won, but nothing is lost. I would rather walk on the water with Jesus. I would rather nearly drown and have to be saved than play it safe and never experience the miraculous.

PURPOSE POINT: Setbacks are just setups for God to show what He is able to do.

TRANSFORMATION MOMENT: When Paul talks about running our race in Hebrews 12, he says to run with "patience," or other translations use the word "perseverance." This suggests it won't be short or easy. There will be setbacks and obstacles on the route, but even when those things trip you up, the race is not over. Success comes through perseverance. If you've been through some tough times, it is time to get back up and try again. Getting out of the boat to walk on water means taking risks.

Peter had to grab hold of Jesus to experience the miraculous. I guarantee you it was worth it. How exhilarating it must have been to walk on water with his Savior! In what areas do you feel the nudge of the Holy Spirit to step out of your comfort zone to accomplish something great?

LIVE YOUR LIFE RELENTLESS (NOT REGRETFUL)

And let us not grow weary while doing good, for in due season we shall reap if we do not lose heart.
GALATIANS 6:9

Several years ago a young man walked up to me and said, "I am getting ready to pioneer a church. Do you have any advice for me?" In fact, he asked, "If you could sum up in one word what it takes to be effective in ministry, what would that word be?" I thought about it a moment, then responded, "Relentless!" You must be a person who is relentless—always abounding in the work of the Lord. If you give up easily, there is no need for you to attempt to accomplish much for God. *Relentless* is a word I use to describe people who will not take no for an answer! They try things one way, and if that doesn't work, they try it another way. But they don't give up. You who are about to break beneath the stress of intense struggles, be relentless! Do not quit!

A terrible thing happens to people who give up too easily. It is called *regret*. It is the nagging, gnawing feeling that says, "If I had tried harder, I could have succeeded." When counseling married couples, I always encourage them to be sure they have done everything within their power to build a successful marriage. It is terrible to lay down at night thinking, "I wonder what would have happened if I had tried this or that." Granted, we all experience some degree of failure. That is how we learn and grow. If a baby had to learn how to walk without falling, he would never learn. A baby learns as much from falling on his bottom as he does from his first wobbly steps. The problem isn't failure; it is when we fail and question if it was our lack of commitment that allowed us to forfeit an opportunity to turn the test into a triumph! We can never be sure of the answer unless we rally our talents, muster our courage, and focus our strength to achieve a goal. If we don't have the passion to be relentless, then we should leave it alone. But, I have a feeling you are a woman of passion who is ready to be relentless.

🐦 **PURPOSE POINT:** *Relentless* is a word I use to describe people who will not take no for an answer! They try things one way, and if that doesn't work, they try it another way. But they don't give up.

🐦 **TRANSFORMATION MOMENT:** How sad it would be to give up on a race and later find out the finish line was just around the bend. Maybe you're running in an intense season and the pressure feels overwhelming. Don't give up. There is a harvest for you to reap wherever you are sowing right now. Keep digging, keep plowing. When you feel weary, stay relentless. If one way is blocked, try another way. When you give your all, you will live relentless, and not regretful.

Maybe there are areas where it feels like you already failed or where you wonder if you gave up too quickly. Invite the Holy Spirit into every past regret. Let Him speak fresh courage over your heart today. Your past is not your present nor your future. It's not too late to be relentless.

SET YOUR GOAL WHERE TALENT AND PURPOSE ALIGN

Many are the plans in a person's heart, but
it is the Lord's purpose that prevails.
PROVERBS 19:21 (NIV)

Multiple talents can be a source of confusion. People who are effective at only one thing have little to decide. At this point let me distinguish between talent and purpose. You may have within you a multiplicity of talent. But if the Holy Spirit gives no direction in that area, it will not be effective. Are you called to the area in which you feel talented? On the other hand, consider this verse: *"And we know that all things work together for good to those who love God, to those who are the called according to His purpose"* (Rom. 8:28). So then you are called according to His purpose and not your talents. You should have a sense of purpose in your ministry and not just talent. Follow the Holy Spirit and set your goals where purpose and talents align.

You would be surprised to know how many people there are who never focus on a goal. They do several things haphazardly without examining how forceful they can be when they totally commit themselves to a cause. The difference between the masterful and the mediocre is often a focused effort. On the other hand, mediocrity is masterful to persons of limited resources and abilities. So in reality, true success is relative to ability. What is a miraculous occurrence for one person can be nothing of consequence to another. A person's goal must be set on the basis of his ability to cultivate talents and his agility in provoking a change.

I often wonder how far my best work is in front of me. I am convinced that I have not fully developed my giftings. But, I am committed to the cause of being. "Being what?" you ask. I am committed to being all that I was intended and predestined to be for the Lord, for my family, and for myself. How about you—have you decided to roll up your sleeves and go to work? Remember, effort is the bridge between mediocrity and masterful accomplishment!

PURPOSE POINT: The difference between the masterful and the mediocre is often a focused effort.

TRANSFORMATION MOMENT: Everyone has unique talents, resources, and abilities. God placed prophetic destiny in you. As you follow Him, He empowers you to fulfill your predestined purpose. The talents within you bear fruit as you live your purpose. The standard for your life is God's standards. Don't compare your life to anyone else. What did He have in mind when He created you? What are you graced to do? When you set goals according to your purpose and ability, you become masterful in the Kingdom.

Make a list of your talents. What areas come easy for you? Ask the Holy Spirit to show you how your abilities align with God's purposes for your life. Spend time praying about this topic and set a goal with the Lord in this direction. As you commit and focus, you'll experience masterful accomplishment!

You're Already Blessed in Your Purpose

No one engaged in warfare entangles himself with the affairs of this life, that he may please him who enlisted him as a soldier. And also if anyone competes in athletics, he is not crowned unless he competes according to the rules.

2 Timothy 2:4-5

Yesterday we looked at talent and purpose. Today we will continue deeper in this theme. I realize that this idea is highly controversial; however, if you are only talented, you may feel comfortable taking your talents into a secular arena. Talent, like justice, is blind; it will seek all opportunities the same. But when you are cognizant of divine purpose, there are some things you will not do because they would defeat the purpose of God in your life! For instance, if it is your purpose to bless the Body of Christ in song or ministry, though you may be talented enough to aspire to some secular platform of excellence, if you are cognizant of your purpose, you will do what you are called to do. Being called according to purpose enables you to focus on the development of your talent as it relates to your purpose!

Whenever we bring our efforts into alignment with His purpose, we automatically are blessed. Second Timothy 2:4-5 says, "*No one engaged in warfare entangles himself with the affairs of this life, that he may please him who enlisted him as a soldier. And also if anyone competes in athletics, he is not crowned unless he competes according to the rules.*" In order to strive lawfully, our efforts must be tailored after the pattern of divine purpose. Everyone is already blessed. We often spend hours in prayer trying to convince God that He should bless what we are trying to accomplish. What we need to do is spend hours in prayer for God to reveal His purpose. When we do what God has ordained to be done, we are blessed because God's plan is already blessed.

🐦 **PURPOSE POINT:** We often spend hours in prayer trying to convince God that He should bless what we are trying to accomplish. What we need to do is spend hours in prayer for God to reveal His purpose.

🐦 **TRANSFORMATION MOMENT:** God has a specific purpose for your life, a beautiful and wonderful purpose. Sometimes we struggle to figure out that purpose. We might do a job or serve in an area because it comes easily based on our talents. Or we might pray for God to bless our goals instead of prayerfully seeking His goals. When we strive in a direction He is not leading, our effort is not lawful. Striving lawfully is when we work toward God's purpose.

Yesterday we prayed and set a goal aligning talent and purpose. Do you feel clarity over your divine purpose or are you still unsure? Keep asking God to reveal His purpose to you. Remember Matthew 7:7, beloved, *"Ask, and it will be given to you; seek, and you will find; knock, and it will be opened to you."* God is faithful to respond, and His plans are already blessed.

THE SAFEST PLACE IS IN THE WILL OF GOD

Lord, how many are my foes! How many rise up against me! Many are saying of me, "God will not deliver him." But you, Lord, are a shield around me, my glory, the One who lifts my head high. I call out to the Lord, and he answers me from his holy mountain. I lie down and sleep; I wake again, because the Lord sustains me.
PSALM 3:1-5 (NIV)

Perhaps you have known times of frustration. Most of us at one time or another have found ourselves wrestling to birth an idea that was conceived in the womb of the human mind as opposed to the divine. For myself, I learned that God will not be manipulated. If He said it, that settles it. No amount of praying through parched lips and tear-stained eyes will cause God to avert what He knows is best for you. I know so well how it feels to find yourself sitting on the side of the bed when you should have been sleeping. I have struggled in the process of anguished surrender. James Taylor had a secular song entitled, "Help Me Make It Through the Night." Those night experiences come to everyone. Those turbulent, boisterous winds of indecisiveness blow severely against the human constitution. The psalmist also shares his testimony in the Scripture, Psalm 3:1-5.

David declares that it is the Lord who sustains you in the perilous times of inner struggle and warfare. It is the precious peace of God that eases your tension when you are trying to make decisions in the face of criticism and cynicism. When you realize that some people do not want you to be successful, the pressure mounts drastically. Many have said, "God will not deliver him." However, many saying it still doesn't make it true.

I believe that the safest place in the whole world is in the will of God. If you align your plan with His purpose, success is imminent! On the other hand, if I have not been as successful as I would like to be, then seeking the purpose of God inevitably enriches my resources and makes the impossible attainable. If the storm comes and I know I am in the will of God, then little else matters.

PURPOSE POINT: I believe that the safest place in the whole world is in the will of God. If you align your plan with His purpose, success is imminent!

TRANSFORMATION MOMENT: In the Old Testament, wars were won through worship. The walls of Jericho fell with a shout of faith. God won these victories Himself as His people trusted and worshiped Him. When we align our plans with His purpose, no matter what comes against us, we are always on the winning side. This doesn't mean things will always be easy. There are still battles to be fought and won, but when we are in His will, we are in the safest place.

Do you feel like you are fighting any battles right now? Does it feel like there are some naysayers in your life saying God will not deliver you? If so, pray the prayer David prayed and know that God will respond. He has the victory for you woman of God.

NO MATTER WHAT, YOU'RE NOT ALONE

My help comes from the Lord, who made heaven and earth. He will not allow your foot to be moved; He who keeps you will not slumber.
PSALM 121:2-3

I remember when my wife and I were raising two children (now we have four). Times were tough and money was scarce. So many were the nights that I languished over the needs in our home. I prayed, or more accurately, I complained to God. I explained to Him how I was living closer to Him than I had ever lived and yet we were suffering with utility bills and lack of groceries. I wondered, "Where are You, Lord!" I was a preacher and a pastor. All the other men of God seemed to have abundance, yet I was in need.

I was preaching, singing, and shouting, but inside the tremors of an earthquake of frustration began to swell. I had been laid off my job, and my church was so poor it couldn't even pay attention. I was in trouble. The gas was off and sometimes the lights. After not being able to pay my bills, I walked out of the utility office and burst into tears. Actually, it was a deluge of sobbing, heaving, quaking, and wailing. I looked like an insane person walking down the street. I was at the end of my rope.

To this melodramatic outburst God said absolutely nothing. He waited until I had gained some slight level of composure and then spoke. I will never forget the sweet sound of His voice beneath the broken breathing of my fearful frustration. He said, in the rich tones of a clarinet-type voice, "I will not suffer thy foot to be moved!" That was all He said, but it was how He said it that caused worship to flush the pain out of my heart. It was as if He were saying, "Who do you think that I am? I will not suffer thy foot to be moved. Don't you understand that I love you?" I shall never forget as long as I live the holy hush and the peace of His promise that came into my spirit. Suddenly the light, the gas, and the money didn't matter. What mattered was I knew I was not alone; the Lord was with me.

🐦 **PURPOSE POINT:** Suddenly the light, the gas, and the money didn't matter. What mattered was I knew I was not alone; the Lord was with me.

🐦 **TRANSFORMATION MOMENT:** In Psalm 121, David writes about the tender help of God. He will not let your foot slip. Even when you sleep, God is not sleeping. He is watching over you day and night. At times, life is challenging. Maybe the pressures of life, with raising children, marriage, financial pressure or any other area, are getting to you. As I shared, during my season of financial struggles, I had restless nights, prayed many prayers, and even broke down in tears.

Right in the middle of one of my hardest moments, God met me. His voice calmed my storm and brought me comfort. I knew I was not alone. God doesn't always change our circumstances right away, but He does meet us with His Presence and His Word.

Read Psalm 121 as you pray today. Ask God to whisper His promises over you once again. You are not alone. Trust me, it will get better!

LIFE COMES IN SEASONS, EMBRACE THEM ALL

For our light affliction, which is but for
a moment, working for us a far more
exceeding and eternal weight of glory.
2 CORINTHIANS 4:17

We will always have seasons of struggles and testing. There are times when everything we attempt to do will seem to go wrong. Regardless of our prayers and consecration, adversity will come. We can't pray away God's seasons. The Lord has a purpose in not allowing us to be fruitful all the time. We need seasons of struggle. These periods destroy our pride in our own ability and reinforce our dependency on the sufficiency of our God. What a shock it is to find that the same person who was fruitful at one period experienced struggle at other times.

When God sends the chilly winds of winter to blow on our circumstances, we must still trust Him. In spite of our dislike for the blinding winds and the icy grip of winter seasons, there is a purpose for these temporary inconveniences. The apostle Paul calls such times *"...light affliction, which is but for a moment..."* (2 Cor. 4:17). I say, "This too shall pass!"

Some things you are not meant to change, but to survive. So if you can't alter it, then outlive it! Be like a tree. In the frosty arms of winter the forest silently refurbishes its strength, preparing for its next season of fruitfulness. Its branches rocking in the winds, the sap and substance of the tree go underground. It is not good-bye, though; in the spring it will push its way up into the budding of a new experience. Temporary setbacks create opportunities for fresh commitment and renewal. If you were to record your accomplishments, you would notice that they were seasonal. There are seasons of sunshine as well as rain. Pleasure comes, then pain, and vice versa. Each stage has its own purpose.

PURPOSE POINT: Temporary setbacks create opportunities for fresh commitment and renewal.

TRANSFORMATION MOMENT: If you feel the chill of winter, take heart daughter, this too shall pass. This is not the full story of your life; it is one season. Psalm 1:3 says, *"He shall be like a tree planted by the rivers of water, that brings forth its fruit in its season, whose leaf also shall not wither; and whatever he does shall prosper."* The same goes for other people. Some people around you are in their spring season, others are in the barren winter. This is one more reason not to compare yourself to others.

If you are in winter, use this season to put your roots deep in God so that you will bear fruit in due time. And don't compare your winter to someone else's spring. Celebrate their fruit and trust that yours is coming too. Ask God how you can celebrate someone today.

DON'T MAKE PERMANENT DECISIONS BASED ON TEMPORARY CIRCUMSTANCES!

For the vision is yet for an appointed time; but at the end it will speak, and it will not lie. Though it tarries, wait for it; because it will surely come, it will not tarry.

HABAKKUK 2:3

One of the greatest struggles I have encountered is the temptation to make permanent decisions based on temporary circumstances. Someone once said, "Patience is a tree whose root is bitter, but its fruit is sweet." The reward of patience is reflected in gradually not having to amend your amendments. Temporary circumstances do not always require action. I have found that prayer brings us into patience. Patience results from trust. We cannot trust a God we don't talk with. Do not misunderstand me; God needs men and women who are decisive. However, every situation shouldn't get an immediate reaction. Prayer is the seasoning of good judgment. Without it, our decisions will not be palatable.

Our struggle is in waiting for the appointment we have with destiny. Perhaps I should first point out that God is a God of order; He does everything by appointment. He has set a predetermined appointment to bring to pass His promise in our lives. An appointment is a meeting already set up. My friend, God did not forget you or your promises. As David declares, "*What is man, that You art mindful of him...?*" (Ps. 8:4). God's mind is full of you. Even in those moments of absolute stagnation in your life, He is working an expected end for your good (see Jer. 29:11).

Through the many tempestuous winds that blow against our lives, God has already prepared a way of escape. Our comfort is in knowing that we have an appointment with destiny. It is the inner awareness that makes us realize that in spite of temporary circumstances, God has a present time of deliverance.

PURPOSE POINT: God is the God of order; He does everything by appointment. He has set a predetermined appointment to bring to pass His promise in our lives.

TRANSFORMATION MOMENT: Beloved, God remembers you. He is the One who created you and tenderly stands by your side in every season as a proud Father. The Bible says that every good gift comes from our Father (see James 1:17). God wants to communicate with you and build a deep trust relationship with you. Part of the process is being patient and believing what God says over and above temporary circumstances. It helps to speak His word aloud. Remind yourself that His mind is full of you! Declare that He is working all things for good.

Ask God to lead you to a Bible verse about His promises to you. Declare aloud what He shows you. If you aren't sure, start with the verses I've referenced here: Hab 2:3; Ps. 8:4; Jer. 29:11; James 1:17.

NOT BY MIGHT, NOR BY POWER, BUT BY GOD'S SPIRIT

So he answered and said to me: "This is the word of the Lord to Zerubbabel: 'Not by might nor by power, but by My Spirit,' says the Lord of hosts."
ZECHARIAH 4:6

We are enveloped in peace when we know that nothing the enemy does can abort the plan of God for our lives. Greater still is the peace that comes from knowing we cannot rush God's timing. When the Lord speaks a word into our lives, it is like a seed. It takes time for a seed to sprout. God knows when we have reached the time of germination. Our confidence is in God's seed. When the promise has grown in the fertile ground of a faith-filled heart and reached the time of maturation, it will come to pass. It will be a direct result of the presence of God. It will not be by human might or power, but by the Spirit of the Lord (see Zech. 4:6).

The psalmist David said, *"My times are in Your hand"* (Ps. 31:15a). For me there is a sense of tranquility that comes from resting in the Lord. His appointment for us is predetermined.

There is a peace that comes from knowing God has included us in His plan—even the details.

I earnestly believe that everyone is predestined to accomplish certain things for the Lord. Somewhere in the recesses of your mind there should be an inner knowing that directs you toward an expected end. For me, it is this awareness that enables me to push myself up out of the bed and keep fighting for survival. You must be the kind of tenacious person who can speak to the enemy and tell him, "My life can't end without certain things coming to pass. It's not over until God says, 'It's over!'"

🕊 **PURPOSE POINT:** Our confidence is in God's seed. When the promise has grown in the fertile ground of a faith-filled heart and reached the time of maturation, it will come to pass.

🕊 **TRANSFORMATION MOMENT:** No matter what happened in your past, God still has a good plan for your life. He predestined you to accomplish certain things. Paul puts it this way: *"For we are His workmanship, created in Christ Jesus for good works, which God prepared beforehand that we should walk in them"* (Eph. 2:10). God is the One who leads you into those purposes. Nothing can stop the Lord. Your times are in His hands. His Spirit, not human power, brings the victory. All of these truths should bring deep peace to your heart. Don't let the enemy lie to you. It's not over!

Invite the Holy Spirit to remind you of the purposes God has for your life. What resonates in your heart with that "inner knowing"? What gives you strength to keep going forward?

"TRUTH SMASHED DOWN TO THE GROUND WILL RISE AGAIN UNDAUNTED!"

And we know that all things work together
for good to those who love God, to those who
are the called according to His purpose.

ROMANS 8:28

Twice in my childhood I spoke prophetically about things that have since come to pass. I don't know how, at that early age, I knew I had an appointment with destiny, but I somehow sensed that God had a purpose for my life. I can't say that everything I encountered in life pushed me toward my destiny though. On the contrary, there were sharp contradictions as I went through my tempestuous teens. Still, I had that inner knowing, too deep to be explained.

I want you to know that even if circumstances contradict purpose, purpose will always prevail! It is the opposition that clearly demonstrates to you that God is working. If the fulfillment of the prophecy was without obstruction, you would assume you had merely received serendipity. However, when all indicators say it is impossible and it still occurs, then you know God has done it again.

Perhaps your child is veering away from what you believe to be his predestined end. Maybe he or she is having stormy teenage years. Let me share a quote with you. Dr. Martin Luther King Jr. is noted to have paraphrased William Cullen Bryant this way: "Truth smashed down to the ground will rise again undaunted!" It may seem impossible, but God knows how to make all things work together for good to them that love the Lord (see Rom. 8:28). It is so important for parents to instill a sense of destiny in their children. Once they realize that they have immeasurable potential, there is no stopping them. I am not saying that they won't deviate from the path—all of us have done that. But thank God they have been given a path to deviate from. Many children today don't know what the path even looks like. When it is all said and done, they will, like the prodigal son, come to themselves!

PURPOSE POINT: If the fulfillment of the prophecy was without obstruction, you would assume you had merely received serendipity. However, when all indicators say it is impossible and it still occurs, then you know God has done it again.

TRANSFORMATION MOMENT: Maybe you had wonderful parents who instilled a sense of destiny into your heart. However, if you never received that, I want you to know that God is your Good Father. He has a path. Throughout your life, He has been speaking dreams and destiny into your heart, whether or not you were aware of His voice. The truths He placed within you will rise. Nothing is impossible for Him. The same goes for your children. Keep praying for them and never give up hope.

Are there any people in your life who are young in age or in their walk with the Lord? Could you be a spiritual mother and speak destiny into their hearts? Ask God to highlight someone to you who might need some extra encouragement in this area.

YOUR PROMISE MAY BE DELAYED, BUT IT CAN'T BE DENIED

Then the Lord said to me, "You have seen well,
for I am ready to perform My word."
JEREMIAH 1:12

In Genesis, the Lord promised Eve a seed. He said, *"And I will put enmity between you and the woman, and between your seed and her Seed; He shall bruise your head, and you shall bruise His heel"* (Gen. 3:15). When Eve produced what she may have thought to be the promised seed, there were real problems. Her eldest son, Cain, was extremely jealous of her younger son, Abel. In the heat of rage, Cain killed his brother. In one swoop of jealousy, all of Eve's dreams lay bleeding on the ground. Now her eldest son was a criminal on the run, and her younger son snuffed out in the prime of life. Bleak despair pressed upon the heart of this mother. She was supposed to be the mother of all living and all she had raised was a corpse and its murderer.

But God unwrapped the blanket of failure from around her and blessed her with another son. His name she called "Seth." *Seth* means "substituted." It comes from the Hebrew root word *shiyth*, which means to appoint or place. Suddenly, as she held her new baby in her arms, she began to realize that God is sovereign. If He decrees a thing, it will surely come to pass. That doesn't stop the evil one from trying to delay the fulfillment of what God has said, but he can't stop it from happening. Your blessing may not come in the way you thought it would. It may not come through the person you thought it would. But if God said it, then rest assured. It may be delayed, but it cannot be denied. Eve called her third son "Seth," for she understood that if God makes a promise to bless someone, He will find a way! Even if it means appointing a substitute, He will perform His promise.

PURPOSE POINT: Your blessing may not come in the way you thought it would. It may not come through the person you thought it would. But if God said it, then rest assured. It may be delayed, but it cannot be denied.

TRANSFORMATION MOMENT: Do you feel like some things in your life didn't go how you hoped they would? Maybe you, like Eve, have experienced painful loss. Or maybe it's a dream or vision that feels dead. Those circumstances can bring us to bleak despair, but nothing catches God by surprise. He knows everything that has happened and will happen in your life. You can trust Him even if things look messy. God will find a way to bless you.

Sometimes we need to let go of our ideas of how things should be in order to see where He's moving. If things didn't go according to plan, ask God for His perspective. Ask Him if there is anything you need to let go of, perhaps a past disappointment, so that you can receive the blessings He has for today.

IF LIFE HAS PUT YOU ON HOLD, HANG ON!

*And Adam knew his wife again, and she bore a son
and named him Seth, "For God has appointed another
seed for me instead of Abel, whom Cain killed."*
GENESIS 4:25

God's purpose was not aborted when Cain killed Abel.
In spite of the fact that life has its broken places,
ultimately everything God has ever said will come to pass.
Have you ever had to go through a time of attack? Satan tries
to assassinate the will of God in your life. Nevertheless, He
who has begun a good work in you shall perform it until
the day of Jesus Christ (see Phil. 1:6). When we suffer loss
like Eve did, there is a feeling of forlornness. However, you
cannot allow past circumstances to abort future opportunity.
If you have experienced loss in your life, I tell you that God
has a way of restoring things you thought you would never
see again.

We come into this world fully cognizant of the fact that
we have a limited amount of time. We don't live here for very
long before we are confronted with the cold realities of death.
From the loss of a goldfish to the death of a grandparent,

all parents find themselves saddled with the responsibility of explaining why the pet or the person will not be coming back anymore. Yet what disturbs me most is not the quantity of life, but the quality of life. Simply stated, when death comes to push me through its window from time into eternity, I want to feel as though I accomplished something worthwhile. I want to feel that my life made some positive statement.

The saddest scenario I can imagine would be to face death's rattling call and wonder what would have happened if I had tried harder. It would be terrible to look back over your life and see that the many times you thought your request was denied, it was actually only delayed. Life will always present broken places, places of struggle and conflict. If you have a divine purpose and life has put you on hold, hang on! Stay on the line until life gets back to you. If you believe as I do, then it's worth the wait to receive your answer from the Lord.

PURPOSE POINT: It would be terrible to look back over your life and see that the many times you thought your request was denied, it was actually only delayed.

TRANSFORMATION MOMENT: Loss is very real and all of us will have to walk through it at certain points in life. The emotions Eve must have gone through were legitimate and valid. One of her sons was gone forever. The other was convicted of murder, which isn't anyone's dream for their child. The heartbreak would have gone very deep. If you've suffered loss or disappointment, take the time to grieve. Let

God meet you in that situation and heal your heart, beloved, but don't stay there.

God has promises over your life that will not be denied. Let Him take you by the hand and lead you into the next season. He is tender with your heart. Spend time inviting the Holy Spirit into your disappointment or loss today. Ask God for fresh hope for your good and beautiful future.

HAVE THE FAITH TO ASSUME A HOLDING PATTERN

*I waited patiently for the Lord; and He inclined to
me, and heard my cry. He also brought me up out of
a horrible pit, out of the miry clay, and set my feet
upon a rock, and established my steps. He has put
a new song in my mouth--praise to our God; many
will see it and fear and will trust in the Lord.*
PSALM 40:1-3

The real test of faith is in facing the silence of being on
hold. Those are the suspended times of indecision. Have
you ever faced those times when your life seemed stagnant?
Have you felt you were on the verge of something phenomenal,
that you were waiting for that particular breakthrough that
seemed to be taunting you by making you wait? All of us
have faced days that seemed as though God had forgotten
us. These are the moments that feel like eternity. These
silent coaches take your patience into strenuous calisthenics.
Patience gets a workout when God's answer is no answer. In
other words, God's answer is not always yes or no; sometimes
He says, "Not now!"

It is God's timing that we must learn. He synchronizes His answers to accomplish His purpose. I wonder if we as the children of God shouldn't be better prepared for those times in our lives when God speaks from His throne, "Assume a holding pattern until further notice." The question is not always, "Do you have enough faith to receive?" Sometimes it is this: "Do you have enough faith to assume a holding pattern and wait for the fulfillment of the promise?"

You feel a deep sense of contentment when you know God has not forgotten you. When working with people, we often must remind them that we are still there. They seem to readily forget who you are or what you did. God doesn't! Don't confuse your relationship with Him with your relationship with people. God says, through Paul, that it is unrighteous to forget. *"For God is not unjust to forget your work and labor of love which you have shown toward His name, in that you have ministered to the saints, and do minister"* (Heb. 6:10). God simply doesn't forget.

PURPOSE POINT: God's answer is not always yes or no; sometimes He says, "Not now!" It is God's timing that we must learn. He synchronizes His answers to accomplish His purpose.

TRANSFORMATION MOMENT: Do you remember long road trips as a child? Or maybe you have children and car rides feel eternally long. Life can feel like that too when we're waiting for something we really want, but don't have yet. Children ask the question: "Are we there yet?" repeatedly until finally the destination is reached. We can be like that too, continuously reminding God that we are still down here waiting. But, my daughter, God did not forget you.

You might feel like life is stagnant and you have no answers, but God is never stagnant. He is always working on your heart and orchestrating situations to fulfill His purposes in you and for you. Rest in Him and ask Him to teach you about His perfect timing.

GOD REMEMBERED NOAH AND HE REMEMBERS YOU TOO

But God remembered Noah and all the wild animals and the livestock that were with him in the ark, and He sent a wind over the earth, and the waters receded.

GENESIS 8:1 (NIV)

I will never forget the time I went through a tremendous struggle. I thought it was an emergency. I thought I had to have an answer right then. I learned that God isn't easily spooked by what I call an emergency. While struggling in my heart to understand why He had not more readily answered my request, I stumbled upon a word that brought streams into my desert.

The first four words were all I needed: *But God remembered Noah.* I still quote them from time to time. When you realize that God knows where you are and that He will get back to you in time—what peace, what joy! Before Noah ran out of resources and provisions, God remembered him! The Lord knows where you are and He knows how much you have left in reserve. Just before you run out, God will send the wind to blow back the waters of impossibility and provide for you.

I can't begin to describe the real ammunition I received out of those four powerful words. When I read them, I knew God also remembered me. I too need ministry to keep my attitude from falling while I wait on the manifestation of the promise of God. Sometimes very simplistic reminders that God is still sovereign bring great joy to the heart of someone who is in a holding pattern. The comforting Spirit of God calms my fears every time He reminds me that God doesn't forget. He has excellent records.

PURPOSE POINT: The Lord knows where you are and He knows how much you have left in reserve. Just before you run out, God will send the wind to blow back the waters of impossibility and provide for you.

TRANSFORMATION MOMENT: God is working at every moment, but there is a much bigger picture than what we see. In Noah's day, God had a very specific plan that made no sense in the natural realm. Noah had to build a giant boat for his family and all the animal species. Imagine what people must have said about him as he worked. He probably felt a little crazy. Then it rained for 40 days (see Gen. 7:12). Noah and his family were in the ark for almost a year! I bet they wondered if those storms would ever end. Maybe they felt forgotten, but then those four words: *But God remembered Noah.*

Oh Beloved, no matter how long the storm has been, God remembers. He will blow back the waters and make a way. Ask Him to for a glimpse into eternity today.

THERE IS A WIND THAT CAN'T BE STOPPED!

When the Day of Pentecost had fully come, they were all with one accord in one place. And suddenly there came a sound from heaven, as of a rushing mighty wind, and it filled the whole house where they were sitting.
ACTS 2:1-2

God has excellent records. His records are so complete that the hairs on your head are numbered (see Matt. 10:30). They are not just counted. Counted would mean He simply knows how many. No, they are numbered, meaning He knows which hair is in your comb! You know He has chronological records of your hair strands. Then you should know He has your family, your tithes, and your faithfulness in His view. How much more would God watch over you, if He already watches the numerical order of your hair?

When Noah had been held up long enough to accomplish what was necessary for his good, God sent the wind. There is a wind that comes from the Presence of God. It blows back the hindrances and dries the ground beneath your feet. The wind of the Holy Spirit often comes as a sign to you from the control tower. You have been cleared for a landing! Whenever the breath of the Almighty breathes a fresh anointing on you, it is a divine indication of a supernatural deliverance.

Regardless of the obstacle in your life, there is a wind from God that can bring you out. Let the wind of the Lord blow down every spirit of fear and heaviness that would cause you to give up on what God has promised you. The description of the Holy Spirit says He is as *"a rushing mighty wind"* (Acts 2:2). For every mighty problem in your life, there is a mighty rushing wind! Now, a normal wind can be blocked out. If you close the door and lock the windows, the wind just passes over without changing the building. But if the wind is a mighty rushing wind, it will blow down the door and break in the windows. There is a gusty wind from the Lord that is too strong to be controlled. It will blow back the Red Sea. It will roll back the Jordan River. It will blow dry the wet, marshy, flooded lands as in the days of Noah. God's wind is still ultra-effective against every current event in your life.

PURPOSE POINT: Let the wind of the Lord blow down every spirit of fear and heaviness that would cause you to give up on what God has promised you.

TRANSFORMATION MOMENT: Throughout the Bible, the Red Sea is mentioned as a reference point to God's miraculous, delivering power. The Israelites were being chased by the Egyptian armies. When they got to the Red Sea, they were terrified. Then God parted the waters. They walked through on dry ground and their enemies drowned. God is mighty to save and strong to deliver. His ways don't usually look the way we expect. When our enemies are chasing us down, fear is very real. Maybe that is why God gave us many examples of His deliverance.

Read Exodus 14 and let it stir up your faith in God's mighty power to deliver you. If you are facing an impossibility, ask God to blow the wind of His Holy Spirit and make a way through the waters.

PEOPLE ARE THE GREATEST INVESTMENTS IN THE WORLD

For God so loved the world that He gave His only begotten Son, that whoever believes in Him should not perish but have everlasting life.
JOHN 3:16

We often face discouragement in this world. Many have never had anyone who believed in them. Even after achieving some level of success in one area or another, many have not had anyone to point out their potential. Isn't it amazing how we can see so much potential in others, yet find it difficult to unlock our own hidden treasure? Highly motivated people are not exempt from needing someone to underline their strengths and weaknesses. It is impossible to perceive how much stronger we might be if we had had stronger nurturing. Nurturing is the investment necessary to stimulate the potential that we possess. Without nurturing, inner strengths may remain dormant. Therefore it is crucial to our development that there be some degree of nurturing the intrinsic resources we possess.

There is a difference in the emotional makeup of a child who has had a substantial deposit of affection and affirmation.

Great affirmation occurs when someone invests into our personhood. I believe that people are the greatest investments in the world. A wonderful bond exists between the person who invests and the one in whom the investment is made. This bond evolves from the heart of anyone who recognizes the investment was made before the person accomplished the goal. Anyone will invest in a sure success, but aren't we grateful when someone supports us when we were somewhat of a risk?

It is impossible to discuss the value of investing in people and not find ourselves worshiping God—what a perfect picture of investment. God is the major stockholder. No matter who He later uses to enhance our characters, we need to remember the magnitude of God's investment in our lives.

PURPOSE POINT: Anyone will invest in a sure success, but aren't we grateful when someone supports us when we were somewhat of a risk?

TRANSFORMATION MOMENT: God created us for relationship and those relationships enhance our life. We fulfill our purposes together. Whether or not you've had nurturing, affection and affirmation from people, remember that Jesus paid the highest price for your life. He believes in you that much. He says you are worth the risk and you're worth investing in.

In the Body of Christ, we have the opportunity to call out each other's potential and help each other discover inner strengths. Investing in people who are "risky" can have the most impact. Like all high-risk investments, there is possibility for a great return. God knows what He placed in each person. Ask Him to show you who is in need of your investment. Who can you affirm and nurture as they work toward their potential?

GOD PLACES HIS PRIZE POSSESSIONS IN THE FIRE

But He knows the way that I take; when He
has tested me, I shall come forth as gold.
JOB 23:10

Although it is true that fire will not destroy gold, it is important to note that fire purifies the gold. When God gets ready to polish His gold, He uses fiery trials. Unfortunately, nothing brings luster to your character and commitment to your heart like opposition does. The finished product is a result of the fiery process. Whenever you see someone shining with the kind of brilliancy that enables God to look down and see Himself, you are looking at someone who has been through the furnace of affliction.

Let me warn you: God places His prize possessions in the fire. The precious vessels that He draws the most brilliant glory from often are exposed to the melting pot of distress. The bad news is, even those who live godly lives will suffer persecution. The good news is, you might be in the fire, but God controls the thermostat! He knows how hot it needs to be to accomplish His purpose in your life. I don't know anyone I would rather trust with the thermostat than the

God of all grace. Every test has degrees. Some people have experienced similar distresses, but to varying degrees. God knows the temperature that will burn away the impurities from His purpose.

God is serious about producing the change in our lives that will glorify Him. He will fight to protect the investment He has placed in your life. What a comfort it is to know that the Lord has a vested interest in my deliverance. He has more than just concern for me. God has begun the necessary process of cultivating what He has invested in my life. Have you ever stopped to think that it was God's divine purpose that kept you afloat when others capsized beneath the load of life? Look at Job; he knew that God had an investment in his life that no season of distress could eradicate.

PURPOSE POINT: Whenever you see someone shining with the kind of brilliancy that enables God to look down and see Himself, you are looking at someone who has been through the furnace of affliction.

TRANSFORMATION MOMENT: If you want to shine brightly, you'll have to go through the fire that purifies your character and commitment. God knows exactly what you need to achieve your full potential. He invested in your salvation, and now He continuously invests in your life. The fires He brings you through are for your good. And He has a vested interest in your deliverance. The same God who leads you into the fire is faithful to bring you out again, purified.

Can you look back on your life and see the good that came out of difficult seasons? Did you learn something about God? Did your character change? If there are any areas of your life that feel under fire right now, ask God to give you clarity and assurance that He has a purpose.

GOD SPARES NOTHING TO INVEST IN OUR LIVES

I indeed baptize you with water unto repentance, but He who is coming after me is mightier than I, whose sandals I am not worthy to carry. He will baptize you with the Holy Spirit and fire. His winnowing fan is in His hand, and He will thoroughly clean out His threshing floor, and gather His wheat into the barn; but He will burn up the chaff with unquenchable fire.
MATTHEW 3:11-12

How often God has had to fan the flames around me to produce the effects that He wanted in my life. It is sad to have to admit this, but many times we release the ungodliness from our lives only as we experience the dread chastisement of a faithful God who is committed to bringing about change. His hand has fanned the flames that were needed to teach patience, prayer, and many other invaluable lessons. We need His corrections. We don't enjoy them, but we need them. Without the correction of the Lord, we continue in our own way.

Hebrews 12:8 (NIV) says, *"If you are not disciplined— and everyone undergoes discipline—then you are not legitimate, not true sons and daughters at all."* The definition from Strong's #G3541 is *"nothos* (noth'os); of uncertain affinity; a spurious or illegitimate son:—bastard." What a joy to know that God cares enough to straighten out the jagged places in our lives. It is His fatherly corrections that confirm us as legitimate sons and daughters, not illegitimate ones. He affirms my position in Him by correcting and chastening me.

Because Father God loves us so much, He spares nothing to invest in our lives. The greatest primary investment He made was the inflated, unthinkable price of redemption that He paid. No one else would have bought us at that price. He paid the ultimate price when He died for our sins. What He did on the cross was worship. According to *Nelson's Bible Dictionary*, the word *worship*, literally translated, means "to express the worth of an object." Normally the lesser worships the greater, but this time, the greater worshiped the lesser. What an investment!

PURPOSE POINT: His hand has fanned the flames that were needed to teach patience, prayer, and many other invaluable lessons.

TRANSFORMATION MOMENT: When we see things from God's perspective and from the truth of who He is, we realize that even the fires are truly for our good. He is a Good Father. He loves us. He spared nothing to invest in our lives, giving His very Son for our salvation. If you are going through what feels like discipline or a refining season, look at it through the lens of a loving Father teaching His child. Your fire is not a punishment. It is an investment into your future.

Invite the Holy Spirit into your fires today. Ask God to soften your heart and show you how tenderly He loves and cares for you. Rest in His Presence as a child allowing your Father to speak value over you.

GOD IS SERIOUS ABOUT HIS INVESTMENT IN YOU!

Most assuredly, I say to you, unless a grain of wheat falls into the ground and dies, it remains alone; but if it dies, it produces much grain.

JOHN 12:24

Let's explore more about the concept that God has an investment in our lives. First of all, no one invests without the expectation of gain. What would a perfect God have to gain from investing in an imperfect man? The apostle Paul wrote, *"But we have this treasure in earthen vessels, that the excellency of the power may be of God, and not of us"* (2 Cor. 4:7). Thus, according to Scripture, we possess treasure. However, the excellency of what we have is not of us, but of God. The treasure is "of" God. That implies that this treasure originates from God. It is accumulated in us and then presented back to Him. No farmer plants a field in the ground because he wants more earth. No, his expectation is in the seed that he planted. The ground is just the environment for the planted seed. The seed is the farmer's investment. The harvest is his return, or more accurately, his inheritance as the outer encasement of the seed dies in the ground. Harvest cost the seed its life.

We are that fertile ground—broken by troubles, enriched by failures, and watered with tears. Yet undeniably there is a deposit within us. This deposit is valuable enough to place us on satan's hit list. In writing to the Ephesian church, Paul prayed that *"the eyes of your understanding being enlightened..."* (Eph. 1:18). One of the things he wanted the people to know is the riches of His inheritance in the saints! Paul challenged them to become progressively aware of the enormity of His inheritance in us, not our inheritance in Him. We spend most of our time talking about what we want from God. The real issue is what He wants from us. It is the Lord who has the greatest investment. We are the parched, dry ground from which Christ springs. Believe me, God is serious about His investment!

PURPOSE POINT: We spend most of our time talking about what we want from God. The real issue is what He wants from us.

TRANSFORMATION MOMENT: You are fertile ground. You have so much potential inside of you. God put treasures in you like seeds, and now He is cultivating those seeds for the harvest of your life. When He decided to invest in you, He already knew what He placed within you. This should give you hope and courage! God believes in you. He knows the riches of His inheritance in *you*. Like a farmer, He is

WOMAN *Thou Art* BLESSED

not intimidated by the work required to cultivate the harvest because He looks forward to all the fruit.

Have you ever thought about God's inheritance in you personally? Have you pondered the fruit of your life that you can offer back to your Creator as a woman of God? Ask God to give you deeper insight into what He is growing in you right now.

THERE'S A FOURTH MAN IN THE FIRE

Then King Nebuchadnezzar was astonished; and he rose in haste and spoke, saying to his counselors, "Did we not cast three men bound into the midst of the fire?" They answered and said to the king, "True, O king." "Look!" he answered, "I see four men loose, walking in the midst of the fire; and they are not hurt, and the form of the fourth is like the Son of God."

DANIEL 3:24-25

Remember the story of the three Hebrew boys in the fiery furnace? When the wicked king placed them in the fire, he thought the fire would burn them. He didn't know that when you belong to God, the fire only burns the ties that bind you. People have said that God took the heat out of the furnace. That is not true. Consider the soldiers who threw the Hebrews into the fire—they were burned to death at the door! There was plenty of heat in the furnace. God, however, controls the boundaries. Have you ever gone through a dilemma that should have scorched every area of your life and yet you survived the pressure? Then you ought to know that He is Lord over the fire!

It has been suggested that if you walk in the Spirit, you won't have to contend with the fire. Real faith doesn't mean you won't go through the fire. Real faith simply means that when you pass through the fire, He will be with you. This thought brings you to an unusual reality. In most cases, if I told you that tomorrow you would be burned alive, but not to worry because I would be in the fire with you, my presence in the dilemma would provide no comfort at all. Yet the presence of the Lord can turn a burning inferno into a walk in the park! The Bible says a fourth person was in the fire, and so the three Hebrews were able to walk around unharmed in it (see Dan. 3).

King Nebuchadnezzar was astonished when he saw them overcome what had destroyed other men. It is quite popular to suggest that faith prohibits trouble. But when I read about these young Hebrew men, I realize that actually, if you believe God, you can walk in what other men and women burn in.

PURPOSE POINT: He didn't know that when you belong to God, the fire only burns the ties that bind you.

TRANSFORMATION MOMENT: Faith does not give you an easy life. More often, the exact opposite is true. The more faith we have, the more fire we can endure. He doesn't spare us from moments that require radical faith and great courage. Moses told the Israelites to be strong and of good courage. He reminded them that God would be with them and never fail them or forsake them (see Deut. 31:6). God goes with us through the Red Sea. He goes into the blazing furnace and preserves our lives. Even in death, Jesus went before us and conquered hell and the grave. He truly is Lord over the fire.

What if God asked you to walk right into a scary and impossible situation? Would you be ready to follow? Remember daughter, He will be right by your side.

THE ENEMY CAN'T CONFINE YOUR CALLING

Then I turned to see the voice that spoke with me. And having turned I saw seven golden lampstands, and in the midst of the seven lampstands One like the Son of Man, clothed with a garment down to the feet and girded about the chest with a golden band. His head and hair were white like wool, as white as snow, and His eyes like a flame of fire; His feet were like fine brass, as if refined in a furnace, and His voice as the sound of many waters.

REVELATION 1:12-15

When John was on the isle of Patmos, he was limited to a cave but free in his spirit (see Rev. 1). Remember, satan may work feverishly to limit the ministry and reputation of God's vessel, but he can never confine the anointing and the call on your life. To the enemy the Lord says, *"Do not touch My anointed ones, and do My prophets no harm"* (1 Chron. 16:22).

In fact, John's predicament on Patmos proves that negative circumstances reveal Christ, not veil Him. While in the dank, dismal, dark caves of persecution, surrounded by the sounds of other abused prisoners, John caught a vision. In his newfound image of Christ, he describes the crisp clarity of a revelation given in the midst of chaos. A crisis can clear your perceptions as you behold His face, looking for answers that will not be found in the confines of the situation.

Every ministry gift will eventually confront the cave of loneliness and the prison of an ostracized situation. Nevertheless, let the jailer beware; our God has a prison ministry. He explodes the walls of impossibility. John wrote that he heard the thunderous voice of the Lord. When the voice of God led to the presence of Christ, John collapsed in the presence of the Lord. A deluge flooded the cave as Christ opened His mouth; His voice sounded as the noise of many waters. In the process of seeking the voice, he encountered seven golden candlesticks. The candlesticks are later revealed as the Church. We need men and women who hear the voice of God before they see the work of God. What good will it do us to polish the candelabra and light the candles if there is no voice of God to cause people to turn aside and see?

🐦 **PURPOSE POINT:** We need men and women who hear the voice of God before they see the work of God.

🐦 **TRANSFORMATION MOMENT:** The answer is Jesus. He says, *"I am the way, the truth, and the life. No one comes to the Father except through Me"* (John 14:6). Jesus is the Way. There is no other way. The "prison" of your circumstances is not eternal truth, it is a temporary situation. Your calling and your anointing cannot be confined or snuffed out by the enemy. When we feel trapped in a "prison" of circumstances we don't like, we have a choice to seek God's face and pursue His voice. He has something to say to you right now.

Jesus wants to encounter you. Seek His face beloved. Spend time waiting on His voice. Let it wash over you like rushing waters. Before you seek to do the work of God, listen to the voice of God.

HIS FEET HAVE BEEN IN THE FIRE

Looking unto Jesus, the author and finisher of
our faith, who for the joy that was set before Him
endured the cross, despising the shame, and has sat
down at the right hand of the throne of God.
HEBREWS 12:2

In Revelation, John said that many waters were in Jesus' voice, but the fire was on His feet. Effective communication is always transmitted from the base of burned feet. John said Jesus' feet looked as if they had been in the fire. What a comfort to the indicted character of this Pentecost preacher to find that the feet of his Consoler had been through the fire. Dearly beloved, hear me today: Your Deliverer has feet that have been burned. He knows what it feels like to be in the fire.

I cannot guarantee that you will not face terrifying situations if you believe God. I can declare that if you face them with Christ's presence, the effects of the circumstance will be drastically altered. Seldom will anyone fully appreciate the fire you have walked through, but be assured that God knows the fiery path to accomplishment. He can heal the blistered feet of the traveler.

Thank God for the smoldering feet of our Lord that run swiftly to meet His children in need. But still the question remains, "Is there any preventive protection that will at least aid the victim who struggles in the throes of a fiery test?" If you are in a fiery trial, be advised that it is your faith that is on trial. If you are to overcome the dilemma, it will not be by your feelings, but by your faith. First John 5:4 says, *"For whatever is born of God overcomes the world. And this is the victory that has overcome the world—our faith."* It is the shield of faith that quenches the fiery darts of the devil (see Eph. 6:16). The term *quench* means "to extinguish." If faith doesn't deliver you from it, then it will surely deliver you through it.

🕊 **PURPOSE POINT:** Your Deliverer has feet that have been burned. He knows what it feels like to be in the fire.

🕊 **TRANSFORMATION MOMENT:** Jesus came to earth well aware that He would walk the way of the cross. He did not fear death or persecution, instead He rejoiced in the reward. You are His reward. He was willing to walk through the fire and make a way for you. Maybe those around you don't understand the fires of your life, but Jesus certainly does. It is your faith in Him that will extinguish the fire or get you through it. Are there any fires brewing that you would like to extinguish? Your faith will do the job.

Paul instructs us to take up the shield of faith to quench or extinguish the fiery darts of the devil. Read through Ephesians 6:10-20 today. Put on your armor Mighty Woman of God, and overcome with Jesus.

WHAT DOES FAITH REALLY MEAN?

Who through faith subdued kingdoms, worked righteousness, obtained promises, stopped the mouths of lions, quenched the violence of fire, escaped the edge of the sword, out of weakness were made strong, became valiant in battle, turned to flight the armies of the aliens.
HEBREWS 11:33-34

The fanaticism of some faith theology has intimidated many Christians from faith concepts as they relate to the promises of God. Yet faith is such a key issue for the Christian that the people of the early Church were simply called believers in recognition of their great faith. One thing we need to do is understand the distinctions of faith. Faith cannot alter purpose; it only acts as an agent to assist in fulfilling the predetermined purpose of God. If God's plan requires that we suffer certain opposition in order to accomplish His purpose, then faith becomes the vehicle that enables us to persevere and delivers us through the test. On the other hand, the enemy afflicts the believer in an attempt to abort the purpose of God. Faith is a night watchman sent to guard the purpose of God. It will deliver us out of the hand of the enemy—the enemy being anything that hinders the purpose of God in our lives.

Hebrews chapter 11 discusses at length the definition of faith. It then shares the deeds of faith in verses 32-35a and finally it discusses the perseverance of faith in verses 35b-39. There are distinctions of faith as well. In Hebrews 11:32-35a, the teaching has placed an intensified kind of emphasis on the distinct faith that escapes peril and overcomes obstacles. Christianity's foundation is not built upon elite mansions, stocks and bonds, or sports cars and cruise-control living. All these things are wonderful if God chooses to bless you with them. However, to make finances the symbol of faith is ridiculous. The Church is built on the backs of men and women who withstood discomfort for a cause. These heroes were not the end but the means whereby God was glorified. Some of them exhibited their faith through their shadows' healing sick people. Still others exhibited their faith by bleeding to death beneath piles of stone. They also had a brand of faith that seemed to ease the effects, though it didn't alter the cause.

PURPOSE POINT: Faith is a night watchman sent to guard the purpose of God. It will deliver us out of the hand of the enemy—the enemy being anything that hinders the purpose of God in our lives.

TRANSFORMATION MOMENT: The disciples were Jesus' close friends, men of great faith. Jesus taught them not to worry about anything on this earth, but to store up treasure in Heaven (Matt. 6:20). Faith in Him did not mean an easy problem-free life or becoming financially wealthy. It did mean they learned how to heal the sick, cleanse lepers, raise the dead, and cast out demons (see Matt. 10:8). They received power and the Holy Ghost (see Acts 1). This is the way of faith. You will face opposition, but you will receive power and purpose. Through faith, you will overcome.

Take time today to ponder the true meaning of faith. Read Hebrews 11 to be inspired by powerful testimonies of men and women who walked before you on this road of faith.

WOMAN *Thou Art* BLESSED

ALL PURSUITS ARE WORTHLESS COMPARED TO KNOWING CHRIST

I have been crucified with Christ; it is no longer I who live, but Christ lives in me; and the life which I now live in the flesh I live by faith in the Son of God, who loved me and gave Himself for me.

GALATIANS 2:20

There are times in our lives when God will take us from one realm of faith to another. There are multiplicities of fiery trials, but thank God that for every trial there is a faith that enables us. Christ is the Author and the Finisher of our faith (see Heb. 12:2). He knows what kind of heat to place upon us to produce the faith needed in the situation. Remember, when we present our bodies as living sacrifices, He is the God who answers by fire. The good news lies in the fact that when our faith collapses beneath the weight of unbelievable circumstances, He gives us His faith to continue on. Paul came to the point of truly valuing faith in Jesus above all else:

> *Yet indeed I also count all things loss for the excellence of the knowledge of Christ Jesus my Lord, for whom I have suffered the loss of all things, and count them as rubbish, that I may gain Christ and be found in Him, not having my own righteousness, which is from the law, but that which is through faith in Christ, the righteousness which is from God by faith; that I may know Him and the power of His resurrection, and the fellowship of His sufferings, being conformed to His death* (Phil. 3:8-10).

As the fire of persecution forces us to make deeper levels of commitment, it is so important that our faith be renewed to match our level of commitment. There is a place in God where the fire consumes every other desire but to know the Lord in the power of His resurrection. At this level all other pursuits tarnish and seem worthless in comparison. Perhaps this is what Paul really pressed toward, that place of total surrender. Certainly that is the place I reach toward, which often escapes my grasp, but never my view. Like a child standing on his toes, I reach after a place too high to be touched. I conclude by saying my hands are extended, but my feet are on fire!

PURPOSE POINT: There is a place in God where the fire consumes every other desire but to know the Lord in the power of His resurrection.

TRANSFORMATION MOMENT: Maybe Paul's level of faith resonates completely, or maybe it feels far out of reach. The more you pursue Jesus, the more you will find the things of this world becoming less and less important in comparison. Wherever you are on your faith journey, there is a deeper level to be had. Jesus is the Author and Finisher of your faith, so when you need more faith, simply look to Him. When He sends you fire, remember that His feet are also burning.

Is there anything in this world that competes with your desire for Jesus? Are you willing to let the fire of God purify your heart like gold? Invite the Holy Spirit to take you into deeper faith.

GOD KNOWS YOUR TRUE NAME

And He said, "Your name shall no longer be called Jacob, but Israel; for you have struggled with God and with men, and have prevailed."
GENESIS 32:28

Many of us come to know the Lord because we desperately need to know ourselves. This was true for Jacob, one of God's great heroes. He was a limping leader graced to come to know who he was in a personal way. Jacob wrestled with the only One who can give lasting answers to hard-hitting questions. He wrestled with God!

Jacob's name meant "supplanter" or "trickster," literally "con man." It was only when his trickery brought him to a dead end that he began to struggle with God for an answer. Then he was left alone with God. When we are alone with God, in the isolation of our internal strife, God begins the process of transforming disgrace into grace. It only took a midnight rendezvous and an encounter with a God he couldn't "out slick" to bring Jacob's leg to a limp and his fist to a hand clasped in prayer. *"I won't let You go till You bless me,"* he cries. God then tells him what he really needs to know, that

Jacob is not who he thinks he is. In fact, he is really Israel, a prince. (See Genesis 32:24-30.) Imagine how shocking that would've been. All of his life everyone had called him a trickster morning, noon and night. Jacob simply acted out what everyone had said he was. But with the grip of a desperate man he caught the horns of the altar of prayer and prayed until the Father gave him his real identity. He said to Jacob, *"Your name is Israel, and as a prince you have wrestled with God"* (see Gen. 32:28 KJV).

My friend, when we, like Jacob, seek to know God, He will inevitably show us our real identity. The greatest riches Jacob would ever receive were given while he was alone with the Father. It was simply the Father's telling him his name! If no one else knows who you are, God knows. If you pray, the Father will give you a name.

PURPOSE POINT: Jacob wrestled with the only One who can give lasting answers to hard-hitting questions. He wrestled with God!

TRANSFORMATION MOMENT: For Jacob, understanding and stepping into his true identity took a wrestling match with God in the midnight hour. He did not know who he truly was. He believed the lies spoken over him about being a trickster. He became manipulative and cunning, lying to his own father and stealing his brother's birthright. Maybe you've done some things you aren't proud of and they haunt you. Whatever you've believed about yourself and whatever you've done do not change your true identity. God wants to bring you back into who He created you to be, but that might take some midnight wrestling.

You are a beautiful daughter of God. Ask God to show you what names He speaks over you. These names will bring life, hope and joy even if it takes you some time to believe them.

BE CAREFUL WHO NAMES YOU, WORDS HAVE POWER

The Gentiles shall see your righteousness, and all kings your glory. You shall be called by a new name, which the mouth of the Lord will name.
ISAIAH 62:2

As we discuss this theme of a new name, I want you to understand that it is about identity. Being born again is not a change on your birth certificate; it is a change in your heart. When you are in the presence of God, He will remove the stench of your old character and give you a new one. It is a work of the Holy Spirit. In this sense we have a name change as it pertains to our character. In the Bible names were generally significant to the birth. On other occasions they were prophetic. Jesus means "salvation"; He was born to save His people from their sins. Moses means "drawn out," relative both to origin and prophecy. He was originally drawn out of the water by Pharaoh's daughter, but prophetically called of God to draw his people out of Egypt.

Understand then that a name is important. It tells something about your origin or your destiny. You don't want just anyone to name you. Mary, the mother of Jesus, had the baby, but the angel was sent from the Father to give the name. She couldn't name Him because she didn't fully understand His destiny. Don't allow people who don't understand your destiny to name you.

No one should want just anyone to prophesy over her without knowing whether or not that person is right. Words have power! Many of God's people are walking under the stigma of their old nature's name. That wretched feeling associated with what others called you or thought about you can limit you as you reach for greatness. However, it is not what others think that matters. You want to be sure, even if you are left alone and no one knows but you, to know who the Father says you are. Knowing your new name is for your own edification. When the enemy gets out his list and starts naming your past, tell him, "Haven't you heard? The person you knew died! I am not who she was and I am certainly not what she did!"

PURPOSE POINT: Many of God's people are walking under the stigma of their old nature's name. That wretched feeling associated with what others called you or thought about you can limit you as you reach for greatness.

TRANSFORMATION MOMENT: People called Jacob by his old name. That affected his character and his actions. Those around him didn't see what God saw or recognize the calling on his life. Have people labeled you by your old nature? It might not be a name per say, but rather what they have said about your character or potential. Maybe people have said you won't get very far in life or that your dreams are too big. Maybe they haven't recognized your calling. The enemy also works hard to convince us we will fail or that our past will hold us back from the glorious future God promises. This is why you need to know who the Father says you are.

In prayer, cast off every "old name" and choose to believe what God says! His purpose will prevail. Daughter, you are who He says you are.

RECEIVE IDENTITY FROM YOUR HEAVENLY FATHER AND HEALTHY FATHERS

Even if you had ten thousand guardians in Christ,
you do not have many fathers, for in Christ Jesus
I became your father through the gospel.

1 CORINTHIANS 4:15 (NIV)

When we know what the Father says about us, we know who we are no matter what others say. In the chilly river of Jordan, with mud between His toes, it was the voice of the Father that declared the identity of Christ. His ministry could not begin until the Father laid hands upon Him by endorsing Him in the midst of the crowd. It's so important that we as sons and daughters receive the blessing of our spiritual fathers. I know countless preachers who ran away from their spiritual homes without their fathers' blessings and, even after many years, are still in a turmoil. If Jesus needed His Father's blessing, how much more do you and I? We should not seek to endorse ourselves.

I grew up in a church that had what we called "church mothers." These old saintly women prayed with fire and corrected us with the zeal of lightning. Thank God for the mothers in the Church—but where are our fathers? Many young men and women come into the church desperate for men who will speak into their lives with the unfeigned love of a father. It is important that they have pastors who can lay hands on them and affirm them by giving back to them their identity and self-esteem. Children are nurtured by their mothers, but they receive their identity from their fathers!

We have raised a generation of young men and women who couldn't find their natural fathers and now they struggle with their spiritual fathers. This can also affect our view of God as a Father. But God heals every wound. Allow the hand of your heavenly Father to heal the abuse and neglect of your earthly fathers. God is so wise that He will give you a spiritual father to fill the voids in your life. Trust Him!

🐦 **PURPOSE POINT:** If Jesus needed His Father's blessing, how much more do you and I? We should not seek to endorse ourselves.

🐦 **TRANSFORMATION MOMENT:** You, as a daughter of God, need your heavenly Father's blessing, just like Jesus did. He is the One who defines you and your identity, calling and purpose. If you didn't have a healthy father in the natural, your heart will need to heal from what you lacked. God wants to do a deep work in you. He wants you to know that your past is not your future. Whatever you went through, He wants to fill the voids and bring healing.

If you have not forgiven your earthly father for what you did not receive, take time to do that today. It can be very difficult, but believe me, there is freedom on the other side. Pray for God to bring a spiritual father into your life if you don't already have one. Trust Him in this.

YOU ARE WHO YOUR FATHER SAYS YOU ARE

*And so it was, as her soul was departing
(for she died), that she called his name Ben-
Oni; but his father called him Benjamin.*
GENESIS 35:18

Jacob, now Israel, had many healthy sons, but one birth is marked by tragedy. Rachel, the love of his life, is in the final stages of pregnancy. They are out in the desert rushing to their destination in time, but Rachel goes into gut-wrenching contractions. She births a son; however, this scene is clouded by death who, hovering like a buzzard, stealthily creeps around the bed. Just before death claims another victim, Rachel looks at her baby and names him *Benoni*, which means "son of my sorrow." Then she closes her eyes, and like a puff of smoke in the night, she is gone.

A weeping midwife holds the infant, all that remains of Rachel. Jacob finds his lovely wife gone and his son born. His emotions are scrambled like eggs in a pan. Then he hears the name, "Benoni, son of my sorrow." Jacob's eyes turn deeply within. Perhaps he remembers what a wrong name can do to a child. Whatever the reflection, he speaks with the wisdom that is born only out of personal experience. *"He shall not be called Benoni, son of my sorrow. He shall be called Benjamin, son of my right hand. He is my strength, not my sorrow!"* he declares. Guess whose name prevailed, Benjamin; you are who your father says you are.

No one knew any better than Jacob/Israel the power of a name change! Remember, it was in his Father's presence that he discovered he was not a trickster, but a prince! When you believe on the covenant name of Jesus, you break the strength of every other name that would attach itself to your identity.

PURPOSE POINT: When you believe on the covenant name of Jesus, you break the strength of every other name that would attach itself to your identity.

TRANSFORMATION MOMENT: Psalm 100 says, *"It is He who has made us, and not we ourselves"* (Ps. 100:3b). If you are struggling with knowing who you are, go to the One who created you in your mother's womb. If we have a problem with an appliance, we always refer to the owner's manual. In our case it's the Bible. When repairs are needed, we go to the Manufacturer. He knows everything about you and He knows your true name. He calls you lovely.

In the name of Jesus you must break the spell of every name that would attach itself to you. If your heavenly Father didn't give you that name, then it isn't right. You are who He says you are. Rest in the identity that He places upon you.

WE SERVE THE GOD OF SECOND CHANCES

Therefore God also has highly exalted Him and given Him the name which is above every name, that at the name of Jesus every knee should bow, of those in heaven, and of those on earth, and of those under the earth.

PHILIPPIANS 2:9-10

A good name is a very precious possession. It is often more lucrative than financial prosperity. If your name is associated with wealth, ministry, scandal, etc., then your name soon becomes synonymous with whatever it is most often associated. The dilemma in which many people find themselves ensnared can be put like this: "How can I reverse the image or stigma that has been placed upon my name?" The names of some people are damaged because of past failures and indiscretions. Still others wrestle with the stains of rumors and the disgraceful, damaging, defamation of character.

Whether you have acquired an infamous name through being a victim or a villain, I have good news. If you are wrestling with the curse and stigma of public opinion, if people have categorized you for so long that you have accepted your origin for your prophecy—I still have good news for you. You don't have to stay the way you are. The Potter wants to put you back together again. Do you believe that God is a God of second chances? If you do, I want to unite my faith with yours, because I believe He gives second chances.

This good news is that God changes names. Throughout the Scriptures He took men like Abram, the exalted father, and transformed his image and character into Abraham, the father of many nations. A name is an expression of character; it means no more than the character behind it. There is a place in your walk with God—a place of discipleship— whereby God radically changes your character. With that change He can erase the stigma of your past and give you, as it were, a fresh name in your community—but most importantly, in your heart.

PURPOSE POINT: There is a place in your walk with God—a place of discipleship—whereby God radically changes your character.

TRANSFORMATION MOMENT: For the past several days, we've been working through identity and your new name. As I've mentioned, your name is all about your character and identity, not necessarily a literal name. If you want to fulfill your purpose and receive this new name, you'll have to let God transform your character. Then you'll have to believe in faith whatever God says, even if you don't see it quite yet. Daughter, He knows your future, so you can trust what He says about you. His plans for us are even better than we could ask or imagine (see Eph. 3:20).

I recommend you get on your knees and wrestle with Him in prayer until you can arise knowing what He knows. Rise up from prayer knowing who you really are in the spirit and in the Kingdom.

THE WORD OF THE LORD STANDS ABOVE EVERY OTHER WORD

If that is the case, our God whom we serve is able to deliver us from the burning fiery furnace, and He will deliver us from your hand, O king. But if not, let it be known to you, O king, that we do not serve your gods, nor will we worship the gold image which you have set up.

DANIEL 3:17-18

Many of you are like Hananiah, Mishael, and Azariah. If you don't know them, perhaps you'll recognize them by the heathen names Nebuchadnezzar gave them: Shadrach, "command of Aku," Meshach, "pagan name," and Abednego, "servant of Nego." These names expressed worship to heathen gods, as defined by *Nelson's Bible Dictionary*. Their real names, however, were Hananiah, "Jehovah is gracious," Mishael, "who is like God," and Azariah, "Jehovah has helped." When the wicked king threw them into the fiery furnace, the names God called them prevailed!

There is nothing quite like trouble to bring out your true identity. Aren't you glad that you are not limited to public opinion? God's opinion will always prevail. Those three Hebrews came out of the furnace without a trace of smoke. That old king tried to change the name on the package, but he couldn't change the contents of the heart! Can you imagine those boys shouting when they came out? One would say, "Who is like God?" Another would lift his hands and say, "Jehovah is gracious!" The other would smell his clothes, touch his hair, and shout, "Jehovah has helped!"

If you have agonized on bended knees, praying at the altar to know the purpose and will of God for your life, and His answer doesn't line up with your circumstances, then call it what God calls it! The doctor might call it cancer, but if God calls it healed, then call it what God calls it. The word of the Lord often stands alone. It has no attorney and it needs no witness. It can stand on its own merit. Whatever He says, you are!

PURPOSE POINT: The word of the Lord often stands alone. It has no attorney and it needs no witness. It can stand on its own merit. Whatever He says, you are!

TRANSFORMATION MOMENT: If you are to fight the challenge of this age, then shake the enemy's names and insults off your shoulder. Look the enemy in the eye without guilt or timidity and declare:

"I have not come clothed in the vesture of my past. Nor will I use the opinions of this world for my defense. No, I am far wiser through the things I have suffered. Therefore I have come in my Father's name. He has anointed my head, counseled my fears, and taught me who I am. I am covered by His anointing, comforted by His presence, and kept by His auspicious grace. Today, as never before, I stand in the identity He has given me and renounce every memory of who I was yesterday. I was called for such a time as this, and I have come in my Father's name!"

NEED IS THE FUEL THAT SPAWNS ATTRACTION

So the man gave names to all the livestock, the birds in the sky and all the wild animals. But for Adam no suitable helper was found.
GENESIS 2:20 (NIV)

As we transform and seek purpose, we must examine attractions and relationships. Attractions are allurements that can be based on memories, past experiences, and early associations. It is therefore very difficult to explain the extremely sensitive and fragile feelings that cause us to be attracted. Suffice it to say that we are instinctively attracted to inner needs. That attraction may be based upon a need to be with someone whom we think is attractive, which creates with-in us a certain validation of our own worth, or the attraction may be based on a deeper, less physical value. Either way, need is the fuel that spawns attraction. Opinions on what characteristics are attractive vary from person to person.

Attractions, for many people, can be as deadly as a net to a fish. Seemingly, they can't see that the net is a trap until it is too late. They struggle, trying to get away, but the more they struggle, the more entangled they become. Like drug addicts, they make promises they can't keep, trying to pull away from something that holds them in its grasp like a vise. The key is not to struggle with the thing or the person. The deliverance comes from within and not from without. God is far too wise to put your deliverance into the hands of someone or something that may not have any compassion for you. The victory is won within the battleground of your mind, and its memories and needs.

My children have a remote-control toy car. There's a small apparatus inside the car that is controlled by the remote. If we remove the inner apparatus, the remote won't work. It's the same way with attractions. They evolve and manipulate us only because there is some inner apparatus that makes us vulnerable to them. If the wrong person, place, or thing controls our remote, we are in trouble. We may not be able to stop the person from playing with the buttons, but we can remove the inner apparatus.

🐦 PURPOSE POINT: The victory is won within the battleground of your mind, and its memories and needs.

🐦 TRANSFORMATION MOMENT: The work we've already done on identity will help you to have healthy attractions. The more healed and whole you are, the more your needs are met by God. If you are struggling with attractions that are trapping you in unhealthy relationships (romantic or otherwise), it's time to get free. It's time to take back the remote control. Remember, your deliverance comes from

God, not from another person. He makes you whole. He brings victory in the battlefield of your mind.

Invite the Holy Spirit to show you any relationships where unhealthy dynamics are in play. Every situation is unique, so there is not one right answer. If this is a serious problem for you, I recommend meeting with a mentor or counselor to go deeper in healing and receive more freedom in this area.

CHOOSE RIGHTEOUS COVENANTS

Do not be unequally yoked together with unbelievers.
For what fellowship has righteousness with lawlessness?
And what communion has light with darkness?
2 CORINTHIANS 6:14

We are communal by nature; we have a strong need for community and relationships. However, whatever we are in relationship with, we also are related to. It is important that we do not covenant with someone or something with which we are not really related. Hence, we are forbidden from seeking intimacy, which is a legitimate need, from an inappropriate source. This is a biological law that governs biological order. What was introduced in the shadow of Old Testament theology as a biological law is magnified in the New Testament as a spiritual reality. In the Old Testament, each creature was mandated to bond with its own species. In the New Testament, the believer is commanded not to seek companionship outside the sanctity of the Church. Why? The Church is a species separate from any other, a species of which Christ is the firstborn.

We believers also are told in Second Corinthians 6:14 not to be unequally yoked with unbelievers. We are twice-born people; we are born and then born again. Now, it is not biologically illegal for us to bond with unbelievers; it is spiritually illegal. In the sight of God, yoking ourselves with unbelievers is spiritual necrophilia—having intimate relationships with the dead! Therefore, to be willfully disobedient and choose a companion who you know is dead in the trespasses of sin, is to be involved in spiritual necrophilia. Invariably, if you break a law, you reap a consequence.

I am not referring to those who, while still a sinner, married another sinner, and then were converted. (At that point it is difficult for your partner to bridge the gap because he or she cannot fully *relate* to who you have become.) No, I am concerned for the precious hearts who find themselves attracted to others who haven't had this born-again experience. The person who willingly chooses to ignore God's stop signs is bound to experience adversity. The way of the transgressor is hard; it's not impossible, but quite difficult nonetheless. God's way is the best way. It's not His will for the living to marry the dead!

PURPOSE POINT: The person who willingly chooses to ignore God's stop signs is bound to experience adversity.

TRANSFORMATION MOMENT: First, if you are already in a marriage with an unbeliever, whatever the circumstances, please don't take this as condemnation. There is freedom in Christ no matter what we have walked through. Your purpose in God still stands. Everything we've covered so far is for you too! Keep praying for your husband. I know your prayers are impacting his life whether you see it yet or not.

Now, for those women who are still single, take these words very seriously. Intercourse brings two into oneness. Be very careful what you allow to become one with you. Do not make a covenant with a man who is not born again! God has the very best for you when you follow His commands and His leading. Do not ignore His stop signs!

SIN IS SEPARATION FROM YOUR CREATOR

And you He made alive, who were
dead in trespasses and sins.
EPHESIANS 2:1

As physical death is separation of the spirit and the body, so spiritual death, the state sinners are in, is the spirit of man or woman separated from relationship with his Creator. Like Adam, he is hiding in the bushes of sin and covering himself with the fig leaves of excuses. This verse in Ephesians refers to the fact that sin is in itself a type of deadness of spirit. In the Scriptures, death doesn't mean the cessation of life. It clearly means separation. When a person dies physically, it is not the end of life; it is merely the separation of the body from the spirit. That's why James wrote, *"Even so faith, if it hath not works, is dead, being alone"* (James 2:17 KJV). The Book of Revelation also refers to eternal damnation as the second death! (See Revelation 21:8.) It is called the second death not because existence or consciousness ends, but because it pronounces eternal separation from God. It is the final step of sin. Sin is separation of relationship with God, but the second death is separation from the presence of God!

This concept reminds me of the bone-chilling horror movies we watched as children. By self-inflicted torturous tenacity, a corpse would exhume himself from the grave. These zombies would walk the earth with their hands extended, always searching for but never attaining rest, leaving a trail of victims behind them. That's pretty ghoulish, but it is an accurate description of what sin is: "The Living Dead"! If you're an empty, brokenhearted person walking around always searching for things, for mere tokens of success, then I have a word from God for you. He says, *"I have come that* [you] *may have life..."* (John 10:10b). Accept Him today! Wake up from the nightmare of "The Living Dead" and become a living, loving testimony to the authenticity of the power of God!

When you are in sin, you reach after anything that will numb the pain and help you forget for a few minutes that something is missing. That doesn't work. It's God that's missing—a real relationship with Him. If you are missing Him, you can be reconciled to God at this very moment and receive abundant life!

PURPOSE POINT: Sin is separation of relationship with God, but the second death is separation from the presence of God!

TRANSFORMATION MOMENT: The Bible makes the statement that you were dead in the trespass of sin (see Eph. 2:1). It teaches that all of us were separated from God because of sin. But God has reconciled His people to Himself. Galatians 5:1 (KJV) adds this: *"Stand fast therefore in the* *liberty wherewith Christ hath made us free, and be not entangled again with the yoke of bondage.*" The former days are ended, and the turning point has come. It is time to walk in the freedom Christ purchased for you.

Over the next days, we will go through this topic of freedom from sin and from the past. No matter what your circumstances, Jesus paid for full freedom. Beloved, don't settle for less.

ROMANCING A STONE? I SHOULD THINK NOT!

Brethren, I do not count myself to have apprehended; but one thing I do, forgetting those things which are behind and reaching forward to those things which are ahead.

PHILIPPIANS 3:13

Let's ponder this central concept of avoiding intimate contact with dead things. Consider someone who has lost a loved one, someone whom he or she had once been connected to and involved with. Now the beloved has expired. Who can change what has been done? It is finished. How unthinkable it would be for a grief-stricken widow to spend one final night in trying to move those icy arms into an embrace. Regardless of what the relationship was at one time, surely she would recognize that death changes the reality—not the memory, but certainly the reality. Who would walk past a casket in a funeral home and wink at a corpse? The very idea wavers between being disgusting and hilarious! What type of mind could not grasp the fact that this is inappropriate behavior for intelligent human beings?

If this whole idea is so terrible, and it is, then why would born-again Christians who have been made alive by the power of God, go back into their own past and rummage through the graveyard of circumstances that God says are dead and over with? Why continue to embrace what ought to be buried? Regardless of how alive the event was at the time, when God says it is dead, then it is dead! How strange it must be in the spirit world for you, a living soul, to be wrapped up with a dead issue you have not yet relinquished. There is a spirit of necrophilia eating at the hearts of many Christians. It is not literal, but spiritual. Many wonderful, well-meaning Christians are praising, worshiping, and going to church, but in the stillness of the night, when no one is around, they lie in bed in the privacy of their homes, pull out guilt, scars, and memories, and play with the dead. If it's dead—and it is—then bury it!

Some things might never get resolved, but everything that will not be healed must be forsaken. Really, to forsake it is to forget it. You cannot live in an intertwining embrace with something that God says you are to reckon as dead! Do not yield your body, your time, or your strength to this phantom lover! Tell that old corpse, "You can't touch this!"

🕊 PURPOSE POINT: Regardless of how alive the event was at the time, when God says it is dead, then it is dead!

🕊 TRANSFORMATION MOMENT: I say it's time to admit it, quit it, and forget it! That's all you can do with the past, regardless of what it was or even who was at fault. Forgetting the past means that you release the pain from the memory. You cannot continue to live in or be filled with the past. It is dead and over; break away from the intimate contact it would have on your life. The link that keeps you tied to what is past must be broken.

Take time in prayer today to invite the Holy Spirit to bury the dead. I agree with you right now in the name of Jesus that those unsettled and unsettling issues that keep holding you in the night and affecting you in the light are broken by the power of God.

RECEIVE YOUR FREEDOM HERE AND NOW

Likewise you also, reckon yourselves to be dead indeed to sin, but alive to God in Christ Jesus our Lord. Therefore do not let sin reign in your mortal body, that you should obey it in its lusts. And do not present your members as instruments of unrighteousness to sin, but present yourselves to God as being alive from the dead, and your members as instruments of righteousness to God.

ROMANS 6:11-13

Thank God for the transparent testimony of the apostle Paul when he confided that all of his old issues were not yet laid to rest. There were moments when he was torn between who he wanted to become and who he used to be. Thank God for an honest testimony. We always tell how we came out, but we say nothing at all about how we went through! Paul, however, wasn't afraid of that pharisaical spirit that causes guilty men to be judgmental. He just said it plainly: "I am struggling with an old ghost that I want to be free from." Thank you, Paul, from all the rest of us would-be great men and women who thought there would be no struggle. Thanks for warning us—no, comforting us—with the honesty of your human aggravations.

In Paul's day, there was a gruesome, bizarre punishment for murder: the body of the murdered victim was tied to the murderer. Everywhere the murderer went, the corpse did too, for it was attached to him. He could not forget his victim. The odor of decomposing, deteriorating flesh would reek with the stench of rot, contaminating all of life's moments with the ever-present aroma of decadence. What could we enjoy in life with this flesh hanging on as a sentinel from the past? That's exactly how Paul felt about the old nature that continued to press in so closely to his existence—rubbing him, touching him, always reminding him of things he could neither change nor eradicate.

Eventually, for the punished murderer, this dead, mushy flesh would pass its fungus and disease to him until he died from this association with the dead. What an agonizing, disgusting way to die. When the apostle realized that his association with his past was affecting his present, he cried out, *"O wretched man that I am! Who shall deliver me from so great a death?"* That "who" rang throughout the heavenlies, searched the angels, and found no one worthy to answer the call. That "who" searched the underworld and found no one. It searched the earth—past, present, and future—and found a bleeding Lamb and an empty tomb. Then the angels cried, "Worthy is the Lamb! He is so worthy. Let Him untie you from this curse and be healed!"

🕊 **PURPOSE POINT:** When the apostle realized that his association with his past was affecting his present, he cried out, "*O wretched man that I am! Who shall deliver me from so great a death?*"

🐦 **TRANSFORMATION MOMENT:** You can live with those dead things hanging and clinging to you no better than Paul could. Allow the transforming power of God to rush through your life and cut the cord between you and your past. Whatever you do, remember to get rid of the old body. If the past is over, there is no need for you to walk around with mummies on your back—or should I say, on your mind! This is the time for an epitaph, not a revival. There are some things in life you will want to revive, but not this one. The past is something you want to die.

Jesus is the One found worthy. He can untie you from the past and set you free. Invite Him into every painful place that's still latching on like that dead body. Receive your freedom here and now.

KISS YOUR OLD GHOSTS GOODBYE!

Pharaoh's chariots and his army He has cast into the sea; His chosen captains also are drowned in the Red Sea. The depths have covered them; they sank to the bottom like a stone.

EXODUS 15:4-5

There are some things you would like to have removed extremely far away. There are things I would like to lay to rest in such a definite way that they become merely fleeting wisps of fog faintly touching the recesses of the mind—gone, over, finished! It is those dearly departed, ghostly, painful issues of which I wrote over these past days. Suppose you took for a casket the truths discussed so far, tossed all your concerns into the framework of God's Word, and committed to the ground everything that held you back from being healed and made whole. These phantom assassins are not to be trifled with; they must be laid to rest! This funeral, my friend, is not for them—it is you who must know it's over. Mark down this day as a record that it was this day you put away your nighttime playmates and moved into abundant life. Gather together all those villainous ghosts that desecrate the sanctity of what God would do in your life. Examine them. Cry if need be; scream if necessary—but when the service is over, bury every incident in the freshly turned soil of this word from God. Know that God has delivered you from playing with *dead* things.

In light of all that you have survived, it is high time that the presence of God envelop you in a warm embrace and that the grace of understanding brush your lips with the kiss of peace in the night. You need to be like Jesus who dropped His head in the locks on His shoulders and said, *"It is finished!"* (See John 19:30.) It is time for that kind of benediction to be said in your life. Allow the God of all grace to give you the final rights that forever exorcise the dead from their secret place of intimate contact with you. You have the power. If you're finished with where you were, and you're ready for where you're about to go, then kiss your old ghosts good night. No, better still, kiss them goodbye. Their grasp is broken and you will see them no more.

PURPOSE POINT: Suppose you took for a casket the truths discussed so far, tossed all your concerns into the framework of God's Word, and committed to the ground everything that held you back from being healed and made whole.

TRANSFORMATION MOMENT: When the Israelites left Egypt, they were pursued by their strong, fierce enemies. As they ran, their hearts were probably pounding. When they got to that Red Sea moment, they truly thought they were about to die (see Ex. 14:11). They saw no way of escape.

Sometimes our past pursues us like those soldiers, making us believe freedom is impossible. That is simply not true. Just like God parted the raging waters, He has a way prepared for you. Walk to the other side and leave your enemies to drown and die in those waters.

Why not write down some of these issues that are holding you back on little pieces of paper. Imagine the casket of the truth and toss each one inside. Maybe you want to rip them apart or flush them down the drain. Whatever you do, don't pick them up again!

YOU'VE GOT THE POWER (OVER YOUR MIND)!

For His anger is but for a moment, His favor is for life; weeping may endure for a night, but joy comes in the morning.
PSALM 30:5

Since we have succeeded in destroying our relationships with the past, let's deal with all those side effects that resulted from our previous infidelities. These offsprings of another time when we were less spiritually mature cannot be allowed to exist in us. For instance, jealousy is the child of low self-esteem. Then there is always little tiny suicide wrapped in a blanket hiding in the shadows, born in the heart of a person who has been lying in bed with despair or guilt. Then there are people who habitually lie because fantasy seems more exciting than reality. Promiscuity, the child of a twisted need, has an insatiable appetite like that of greed's, which devours all whom it can touch. For all this, you weep through the night. But David said that if we could hold out, joy comes in the morning (see Ps. 30:5).

Let the hungry mouth of failure's offspring meet the dry breast of a Christian who has determined to overcome the past. Allow the joy of the morning light to push away any unwanted partners, curses, or fears that stop you from achieving your goal. In order for these embryos of destruction to survive, they must be fed. They feed on the fears and insecurities of people who haven't declared their liberty. The parent is dead; you have laid him to rest, but if not destroyed, the residue of early traumas will attach itself to your successes and abort your missions and goals. It nurses itself in your thought life, feeding off your inner struggles and inhibitions.

Once you realize that you are the source from which it draws its milk, you regain control. Put that baby on a fast! Feed what you want to live and starve what you want to die! Anything you refuse to feed will eventually die. You could literally starve and dehydrate those crying, screaming childhood fears into silence, security, and successful encounters. It's your milk—it's your mind! Why not think positively until every negative thing that is a result of dead issues turns blue and releases its grip on your home and your destiny? You've got the power!

PURPOSE POINT: The parent is dead; you have laid him to rest, but if not destroyed, the residue of early traumas will attach itself to your successes and abort your missions and goals.

TRANSFORMATION MOMENT: In the last section, we worked through putting the past to rest, but there can be progeny born in us from our relationships with the past. They must be sought out and destroyed. Lingering negative mindsets that come from past traumas won't help you fulfill your purpose in God. Like a horseleech, they are always sucking the life, excitement, and exuberance out of precious moments. Paul teaches that we must take every thought captive (see 2 Cor. 10:5). It's your mind beloved. You get to choose what lives there.

Are there any troubling thoughts or emotions that come up over and over again in your life? Are there specific topics that feel like horseleeches stealing your joy? Take some time to list these and choose to starve them out!

THINK ON THESE THINGS

*Be anxious for nothing, but in everything by prayer
and supplication, with thanksgiving, let your requests
be made known to God; and the peace of God, which
surpasses all understanding, will guard your hearts
and minds through Christ Jesus. Finally, brethren,
whatever things are true, whatever things are noble,
whatever things are just, whatever things are pure,
whatever things are lovely, whatever things are of
good report, if there is any virtue and if there is
anything praiseworthy—meditate on these things.*
PHILIPPIANS 4:6-8

In this final summation of Pauline wisdom is some wonderful
food for thought. We see that prayer produces the offspring
of peace. This isn't just any peace; it is the peace of God that
stands guard over the spirits and hearts of people like a night
watchman keeping us from hysteria in a crisis. The apostle
Paul swelled to a theological crescendo in verse 8 as he began
to teach thought modification with specific instruction about
what to think upon.

People who are filled with excellence achieve that excellence by the thoughts they have about themselves and about
the world around them. Thoughts are powerful. They feed

the seeds of greatness that are in the womb of our minds. They also can nurse the negative insecurities that limit us and exempt us from greatness. There is a virtue that comes from tranquil, peaceful thoughts that build positive character in the heart. As a rule, people who are cynical and vicious tend to be unsuccessful. If they are successful, they don't really feel their success because their cynicism robs from them the sweet taste of reward.

Thoughts are secrets hidden behind quick smiles and professional veneers. They are a private world that others cannot invade. None of us would be comfortable at having all our thoughts played aloud for the whole world to hear. Yet our thoughts can accurately forecast approaching success or failure. No one can hear God think, but we can feel the effects of His thoughts toward us. Like sprouts emerging from enriched soil, our words and eventually our actions push through the fertilized fields of our innermost thoughts. Like our Creator we deeply affect others by our thoughts toward them.

PURPOSE POINT: Thoughts are powerful. They feed the seeds of greatness that are in the womb of our minds.

TRANSFORMATION MOMENT: This verse from Philippians is incredibly significant. We all need peace that passes understanding instead of swirling thoughts that keep us from greatness. Yesterday you made a list of thoughts and emotions that keep coming up and stealing your joy. It might feel like you have no control over your thoughts, but actually you do. It just takes intentionality and practice.

What would it look like for you to shift your thinking? What if every time one of those nagging thoughts came up you switched gears and thought about something true, honest, just, pure, lovely, or of good report? Try it out starting today. The more you do it the easier it gets.

PULL DOWN THE STRONGHOLDS IN YOUR MIND

*For the weapons of our warfare are not carnal but
mighty in God for pulling down strongholds, casting
down arguments and every high thing that exalts
itself against the knowledge of God, bringing every
thought into captivity to the obedience of Christ.*

2 CORINTHIANS 10:4-5

In my early years of ministry, I had a heartbreaking
encounter. I met a group of children who were physically
or mentally abnormal. Their abnormalities were caused
because their parents were related. These children were the
result of inordinate affections and incestuous relationships!
This plight is unnecessary; it could have been avoided. So
are the children of the mind. You don't have to leave some
grossly deformed generation of problems that beget more
problems! God has given you power over the enemy! He has
given you the power to abort the seeds of failure. Abortion is
a strong term, but effective in this case. Of course, I am not
talking about aborting biological babies, which is wrong. I

am talking about aborting every psychological baby that is growing in the womb of our minds.

These thoughts, wounds, and emotional oddities are self-exalting. They establish themselves as god in your life. They endeavor to control or manipulate you. These progeny of lesser days want to crown themselves as indications of your destiny. How can you afford to submit your future to the discretion of your past? Pull down the strongholds. Pull down those things that have taken a strong hold in your life. If you don't pull them down, they will refuse to relinquish their grip. It will take an act of your will and God's power to stop the spiritual unborn from manifesting in your life. God will not do it without you—but He will do it through you.

The greatest freedom you have is the freedom to change your mind. Enthroned in the recesses of your mind may be some antichrist that would desire to keep you connected to what you have forsaken. Cast it down!

PURPOSE POINT: The greatest freedom you have is the freedom to change your mind.

TRANSFORMATION MOMENT: The Bible says to repent. Repentance is when the mind decides to organize a mutiny and overthrow the government that controlled it in the past. As long as these other things reign in your life, Christ's seat is taken because these thoughts and feelings of the past are sitting on the throne. If they are on the throne, then Christ is on the cross. Put Christ on the throne and your past on the cross. He died for your freedom.

Take time to sit with the Lord and repent of anything that is taking a space on the throne of your mind. Ask Him to help you pull down every stronghold and change your mind. Remember daughter, it's your mind and you have the power!

RAISE UP YOUR HOLY, CALLOUSED HANDS IN PRAISE

Therefore by Him let us continually offer the
sacrifice of praise to God, that is, the fruit
of our lips, giving thanks to His name.
HEBREWS 13:15

In the special moments when thankful hearts and hands lifted in praise come into corporate levels of expression with memories of what could have happened had God not intervened, we find our real ministry. Above all titles and professions, every Christian is called to be a worshiper. We are a royal priesthood that might have become extinct had the mercy of the Lord not arrested the villainous horrors of the enemy. Calloused hands are raised in praise—hands that tell a story of struggle, whether spiritual or natural. These holy hands that we raise unto the Lord are the hands of people who, like Jonah, have lived through a personal hell. Who could better thank the Lord than the oppressed who were delivered by the might of a loving God whose love is tempered with the necessary ability to provoke change.

If we are a priesthood, and we are, then we need an offering. There are many New Testament offerings that we can offer unto the Lord. As an induction into the office of the priest, we offered up our dead issues to a living Christ who quickened the pain and turned it into power! The intensity of our praise is born out of the ever-freshness of our memories, not so much of our past, but of His mercies toward us. The issue then is not whether we remember, but how we choose to remember what we've been through. He is able to take the sting out of the memory and still leave the sweet taste of victory intact. When that happens, we are enriched by our struggles, not limited.

Woe be to the priest who tries to have a fresh worship experience while constantly reliving the dead issues of the past. In that case the memories become an obstacle around your neck. Lift up your head and be blessed in the presence of the Lord. Nothing is nearly as important as ministering to the Lord. What would it matter for all the voices in the earth to harmoniously explode into accolades of appreciation commending you for your contributions, if God disagreed?

PURPOSE POINT: Above all titles and professions, every Christian is called to be a worshiper.

TRANSFORMATION MOMENT: There are so many reasons to praise God. He is worthy of our worship. Before any other purpose or calling He has for us, we are called to be worshipers, priests before Him. This is a lifelong calling, an expression of gratitude and acknowledgment of who He is and all He has done for us. Praising God also drowns out the voice of the enemy. It reminds us of the truth and brings us back to peace, just like in the Philippians 4 passage. Praise is a key to transforming our mind.

Get your favorite worship song playing and minister to the Lord today. Lift your holy hands, calloused as they may be, and thank God that your past is gone, and your future is bright and beautiful.

WOMAN *Thou Art* BLESSED

GIVE YOUR HEART A BATH IN GOD'S WORD

Whoever touches the body of anyone who has died,
and does not purify himself, defiles the tabernacle of
the Lord. That person shall be cut off from Israel. He
shall be unclean, because the water of purification was
not sprinkled on him; his uncleanness is still on him.

NUMBERS 19:13

If we would reach new levels in worship, then we wouldn't be able to touch dead things! Instead they become obstacles that hinder us from deeper experiences in the Lord. In the early Church, the disciples experienced awesome displays of power that we don't seem to experience to the same degree. Few of us are walking in enough light to cast the kind of shadow that causes others to be healed. Our itinerary may take us from church to church, but the disciples traveled in the spirit from age to age and saw things that were not lawful to be uttered! What is wrong? We have become a nation of priests who spend too much time touching the dead and not enough washing our hearts with pure water!

Give your heart a bath. Submerge it deeply into the purity of God's Word and scrub away the remaining debris of deathly ills and concerns. These may be stopping you from participating in the greatest move of God that this generation will ever see! A clouded heart cannot move into the realm of faith. It takes clarity to flow in divine authority. Satan knows that pureness of heart is necessary to see God, to see the will of God, and to see the Word of God. You see, God's will is revealed in His Word. As for the Word, "...*the Word was with God, and the Word was God*" (John 1:1). These distresses and stresses are spiritual cholesterol! They will stop the heart from being able to see God. If the heart cannot see her God, her worship becomes routine and superficial. I can't help but wonder how much more we all would see of God if we would remove life's little buildups that clog the arteries of our hearts and not allow us to see the glory of God.

PURPOSE POINT: Few of us are walking in enough light to cast the kind of shadow that causes others to be healed.

TRANSFORMATION MOMENT: There is so much more available in God than what we are currently walking in. In fact, with God, there is always more. The Book of Acts is not a fairytale, it is a guidebook for the brave followers of Jesus who want to see more! When dead issues take up space in our minds and hearts, it detracts from the purity of our hearts. God's Word is the truth that washes our hearts from all impurities. Trust me, daughter, you don't want to stay cloudy and miss out from participating in the greatest move of God that this generation will ever see!

Get out your Bible and take a few moments (or hours!) washing yourself in God's Word. Pray the verses out loud and let them saturate your heart. Psalm 24 is a great place to start today.

DOES YOUR HEART NEED A LAXATIVE?

Blessed are the pure in heart: for they shall see God.
MATTHEW 5:8

If the priest, the worshiper, has many unresolved issues on her heart, how can she see God? These issues are the obstacles that keep us seeking the wisdom of people rather than the wisdom of God! These are the obstacles that make us feel insecure while we wait for an answer. These are the obstacles that keep many well-meaning Christians needing prayer rather than giving prayer. Let's clean out our hearts and we will hear, worship, and experience God in a new dimension. Clean out every thought that hinders the peace and power of God.

A pure heart is the prerequisite necessary to see God in His fullest sense. He is often described as the invisible God (see Col. 1:15). God's invisibility doesn't refer to an inability to be seen as much as it does to your inability to behold Him. To the blind all things are invisible. How can I see this God who cannot be detected in my vision's periphery? Jesus taught that a pure heart could see God. No wonder David cried out, *"Create in me a clean heart..."* (Ps. 51:10). The term used in

Matthew 5:8 for *pure* comes from the Greek word *katharos*, which means "to clean out," much like a laxative. That may be funny, but it's true. Jesus is saying to give your heart a laxative when you've heard too much or seen too much. Don't carry around what God wants discarded. Give your heart a laxative and get rid of *"every weight, and the sin which so easily ensnares us"* (Heb. 12:1)! What God wants to unveil to you is worth the cleaning up to see.

PURPOSE POINT: Jesus is saying to give your heart a laxative when you've heard too much or seen too much.

TRANSFORMATION MOMENT: From time to time when I minister I have a strange awareness of speaking directly to someone. I feel it now. Whoever you are, get ready for a fresh vision and a new move of God. Shake loose from everything that has kept your heart from seeing God. He is showing Himself. He is not hiding! Clean your heart out and clear your mind; He is there *now*!

Beloved, do not miss out! Be like David who constantly brought everything in his heart before the Lord. He is the prime example of allowing God into the deepest places, into all of his emotions, from distress to sorrow to rejection to joy and praise. He held nothing back and God met him every time. Cry out to God and let Him take you to a new level of revelation.

DON'T LOSE YOUR FIRE, STAY ABLAZE!

Nevertheless I have this against you, that you have left your first love. Remember therefore from where you have fallen; repent and do the first works, or else I will come to you quickly and remove your lampstand from its place—unless you repent.

REVELATION 2:4-5

I often build a fire on those cold wintry nights in West Virginia. Gathering the wood is a small price to pay once the logs have been ignited and that warm, engulfing glow of hot fire begins to reach out from the stove and fill the room with the soothing sound of crackling wood and the slight aroma of fresh fire. On those nights, when the day has taken its toll, I stare into the fire and watch it dance gleefully across the wood like children skipping on a hillside. Bursting up into the air, these occasional eruptions of sparks are nature's answer to fireworks, each group of sparks exploding into neon rainbows of splendor.

While gazing deep into the fire you will notice that the sparks leave the burning log as hot as the fire itself. They swirl into the chimney with an angry ascension into the dark chambers above. But these flickering lights are soon extinguished by no other force than the aftereffects of being separated from their source. I thought, still staring silently into the glowing embers of the next fiery production, "How many Christians explode into the brilliancy of worship and praise, but are soon dark and cold, losing their first fire." Stay in the fire, my friend, where the other embers can share their heat with you and keep you ablaze! It is the fire of God that will assist you in burning up the offspring, the oddities, and the obstacles of yesteryear.

Perhaps that is what happened in the fiery furnace with the Hebrew boys. Yes, there was a fire; I'm not denying that. But the fire was on assignment. It could burn only what was an obstacle hindering those who refused to worship idols from worshiping God. I don't know what they said as they walked around in the flames, observed by the king but preserved by the Lord! Perhaps they were saying what I feel compelled to share with you. Simply stated, some people He saves from the fire; praise God for them. But all too often God saves most of us by the fire!

PURPOSE POINT: How many Christians explode into the brilliancy of worship and praise, but are soon dark and cold, losing their first fire.

TRANSFORMATION MOMENT: In Revelation 2, the church in Ephesus was commended for good works, but they tragically lost their first love. Maybe they were doing the right things, but somewhere inside, they lost their passion for God.

Like those sparks leaping from the fire, they were once bright, but at risk of fading. Even though the fire is not always comfortable, sometimes it is the safest place or it's the testimony that saves someone else. After King Nebuchadnezzar witnessed God's miracle he exclaimed, *"...there is no other God that can deliver like this"* (see Dan. 3:29).

No matter how hot it gets, stay close to the Source. If you feel a little dim or dull, get into His presence and ask Him to ignite your heart yet again.

I DON'T UNDERSTAND WHY, BUT YOU ARE STILL *MY GOD!*

And about the ninth hour Jesus cried out with a loud voice, saying, "Eli, Eli, lama sabachthani?" that is, "My God, My God, why have You forsaken Me?"
MATTHEW 27:46

There are times when it is difficult to understand God's methods. There are moments when discerning His will is a frustrating endeavor. Perhaps we have these moments because we haven't been given all the information we need to ascertain His ways as well as His acts. Many times we learn more in retrospect than we do while in the thick of the struggle. I can look over my shoulder at my past and see that the hand of the Lord has been on me all my life. Yet there were times when I felt completely alone and afraid. Even Jesus once cried out, *"Eli, Eli, lama sabachthani? that is to say, My God, My God, why have You forsaken Me?"* (Matt. 27:46b) Suspended on the cross with a bloody, beaten body, He was questioning the acts of God—but He never questioned His relationship with Him. Jesus says in essence, "I don't understand why, but You are still *My God!*"

I'm sure we have all felt our faith weighed down by a severe struggle that left us wondering what in the world God was doing. I can hardly believe that anyone who seriously walks with God has never felt like a child whose tiny toddling legs couldn't keep up with the strong stride of his parent. Sometimes I've thought, "Daddy, don't walk so fast." We can't see as well or move as quickly. It takes time to develop spiritual dexterity. To remain calm in crises and faithful in frightening times is easier said than done. We need to search for Him.

The search for God is an "equal opportunity" experience for all Christians. Regardless of how successful you may be, you will always have times when you just need to find Him and let Him do a work in you. Consecration is the Siamese twin of sanctification. They are born together and are connected. You can't be consecrated to without being sanctified from. Sanctification sets you apart from distractions, and consecration takes that separated person and quenches his thirst in the presence of the Lord!

PURPOSE POINT: Suspended on the cross with a bloody, beaten body, He was questioning the acts of God—but He never questioned His relationship with Him.

MOMENT: Generally, we see the workings of God when we look back, but while in the throes of the rumbling winds of life, we are often in search of the Lord. Perhaps we are at our best when we are searching for Him. We have no independence, just raw need. There's no dawdling around with things that have no help or healing. Those are the times we know are jobs for God. If He doesn't help us, we will die. Even if His way seems unfamiliar or confusing, press in for your relationship with Father God. Remember daughter, even Jesus wondered why, but He never questioned His relationship with His Father.

Take a moment to just be in God's presence. Leave your wonderings and worries to the side. Just be a daughter in the arms of your Dad who has the whole world in His hands, including your life.

WORSHIP STARTS WITH DESPERATE SEEKING

As the deer pants for the water brooks, so pants my soul for You, O God. My soul thirsts for God, for the living God. When shall I come and appear before God? My tears have been my food day and night, while they continually say to me, "Where is your God?" When I remember these things, I pour out my soul within me. For I used to go with the multitude; I went with them to the house of God, with the voice of joy and praise, with a multitude that kept a pilgrim feast.

PSALM 42:1-4

The search for God is a primary step into worship. We never search for anything we don't value. The very fact that we search for Him indicates that He has become essential to us. There are millions of people who seem to live their lives without noticing that something is missing. They seemingly sense no real void. Our separating ourselves from these ranks and saying, "God, I need You," is a form of worship. The word *worship* stems from the term *worth-ship*. It expresses the worth of an object. The kind of intensity that causes an individual to pursue the invisible in spite of all the visible distractions is a result of need. If we didn't need Him desperately, we could easily be satisfied with carnal things.

God instructs us to seek Him, but not as though He were hiding from us. He is not a child playing hide-and-go-seek. He isn't crouched behind trees giggling while we suffer. The request to seek Him is as much for our benefit as His. When we seek Him, we make a conscious decision

that is necessary for bringing us into the realm of the spiritual. The pursuit of God is rewarding in the development of the seeker's character. Some levels of blessings are never received unless they are diligently sought. It is this seeking after God that often propels Him to perform. If that were not true, the woman with the issue of blood would never have been healed. Her conscious decision to seek the impossible released the invisible virtue of God.

There are no manuals that instruct us step by step as to the proper way to seek the Lord. Like lovemaking, the pursuit is spontaneous and individually conceived out of the power of the moment. Some seek Him quietly, with soft tears falling quietly down a weary face. Others seek Him while walking the sandy beaches of a cove, gazing into the swelling currents of an evening tide. Some would raise their hands and praise and adore Him with loving expressions of adoration. There are no rules—just that we seek Him with our whole hearts.

🕊 PURPOSE POINT: The search for God is a primary step into worship. We never search for anything we don't value. The very fact that we search for Him indicates that He has become essential to us.

🕊 **TRANSFORMATION MOMENT:** The woman with the issue of blood knew what it was to be desperate. The twelve years of suffering and disappointment would have been confusing. I'm sure she cried out to God many times. But yet, she didn't give up. She sought after Jesus. She pushed through crowds and grabbed the hem of His garment, believing in faith for her healing (see Matt. 9:20-2). Maybe you can relate to her struggle. Maybe there is something you've been crying out for year after year without seeing the result and you're weary. Trust me, dear daughter, God has not forgotten about you. In your seeking, you are truly being transformed. He sees your seeking and He has compassion for you.

Let your desperation draw you even closer. Even if you've done it time and time again, invite the Holy Spirit right into this confusing area again today.

CALL AN A.P.B. AND GO ON AN ALL-OUT GOD-HUNT

Seek the Lord while He may be found, call upon Him while He is near. Let the wicked forsake his way, and the unrighteous man his thoughts; let him return to the Lord, and He will have mercy on him; and to our God, for He will abundantly pardon.
ISAIAH 55:6-7

We are like blind people when it comes to spiritual issues; we are limited. Like groping fingers extended in the night trying to compensate for a darkened vision, we feel after God. We feel after His will and His ways. I'm amazed at all the people who seem to always know everything God is saying about everything. In the hymn "My Faith Looks Up to Thee," Ray Palmer and Lowell Mason wrote, "My faith looks up to thee, Oh lamb of calvary, savior divine." My faith looks up because my eyes can't always see. On the other hand, there is a healthy reaction that occurs in blindness; our senses become keener as we exercise areas that we wouldn't normally need.

God knows what it will take to bring us to a place of searching. He knows how to stir us from our tranquil and comfortable perching position of supremacy. There are times when even our great sages of this age murmur in the night. When the congregants have gone home and the crowd dissipates, there are moments in which even our most profound, articulate leaders grope in the dark for the plan and purpose of God. In spite of our strong gait and stiff backs, in spite of our rigid posture and swelling speech, behind the scenes we tremble in our hearts at the presence of God whose sovereign will often escapes the realm of our human reasoning.

Searching releases answers. The Word declares, *"Seek, and you will find"* (Matt. 7:7b). Seeking God takes focus and determination. Many things available to us will not be found without an all-out search. But who knows what God will release if we go on an all-out God-hunt.

PURPOSE POINT: Many things available to us will not be found without an all-out search. But who knows what God will release if we go on an all-out God-hunt.

TRANSFORMATION MOMENT: Our search for God has to be what the police call an A.P.B., an "all points bulletin." All of the department is asked to seek the same thing. Thus our search can't be a distracted, half-hearted curiosity. There must be something to produce a unified effort to seek God. Body, soul, and spirit—all points—seeking the same thing. There is a blessing waiting for us. It will require an A.P.B. to bring it into existence, but it will be worth attaining.

Are you searching for God or have you grown weary? If your eyes can't see right now, look up with your faith. Ask God for fresh focus today. There is an answer waiting for you on the other side of your all-out search!

WHERE WILL YOU TURN IN A CRISIS?

*Then Job answered the Lord and said: "I know that
You can do everything, and that no purpose of Yours
can be withheld from You. You asked, 'Who is this
who hides counsel without knowledge?' Therefore
I have uttered what I did not understand, things
too wonderful for me, which I did not know."*
JOB 42:1-3

I believe there are times when we grow weary of human answers. The crucial times that arise in our lives require more than good advice. We need a word from God. There are moments when we need total seclusion. We come home from work, take the telephone receiver off the hook, close the blinds, and lie before God for a closer connection. In Job's case, he was going through an absolute crisis. His finances were obliterated. His cattle, donkeys, and oxen were destroyed. His crops were gone. In those days it would be comparable to the crash of the stock market. It was as if Job, the richest man, had gone bankrupt. What a shock to his system to realize that all are vulnerable. It is sobering to realize that one incident, or a sequence of events, can radically alter our lifestyles.

Through his financial devastation, Job probably could have reached out to his children for comfort, but he had lost them too. His marriage had deteriorated to the degree that Job said his wife abhorred his breath (see Job 19:17). Then he also became ill. Have you ever gone through a time in your life when you felt you had been jinxed? Everything that could go wrong, did! Frustration turns into alienation. So now what? Will you use this moment to seek God or to brood over your misfortune? With the right answer, you could turn the jail into a church!

In your hardest season, you have two choices. You can turn towards God or turn away. You can become desperate and seek God or become bitter and blame God. After losing her husband and sons, Naomi told people to call her "Mara," which means bitter (see Ruth 1:20-21). She blamed God and let her heart grow bitter. Even so, God still turned everything around and blessed her life. Daughter, stretch out your hands to reach after Him. Don't let bitterness overtake you. Cry out to God. Whatever you do, do not allow this moment to pass you by!

PURPOSE POINT: Will you use this moment to seek God or to brood over your misfortune?

TRANSFORMATION MOMENT: We are all limited, and we all go through challenging seasons. However, when there is a strong desire, we overcome our inabilities and our circumstances, to press our way into His presence. As we talked about yesterday, those who seek shall find (see Matt. 7:7b).

That is a promise. Job struggled and cried and complained. His friends couldn't even help him in that moment. He lost everything, and he was a desperate man. Naomi also lost everything. And yet God had another season of blessing on the other side of their all-out searchs.

Maybe you feel you've lost everything too. If you don't know where to start just reach out your hands to the only One who knows the end from the beginning. Make a choice to turn towards Him and not away. Don't miss this chance to give an offering of praise. God sees your sacrifice.

GOD HAS A SET TIME TO BLESS YOU; JUST HOLD ON

"Look, I go forward, but He is not there, and backward, but I cannot perceive Him; when He works on the left hand, I cannot behold Him; when He turns to the right hand, I cannot see Him."
JOB 23:8-9

Comfort comes when you know that the present adversity will soon be over. But what comfort can be found when it seems the problem will never cease? Job said, *"Look, I go forward, but He is not there"* (Job 23:8a). It is terrifying when you see no change coming in the future. Job was saying, "I see no help, no sign of God, in the future." It actually is satan's trick to make you think help is not coming. That hopelessness then produces anxiety. On the other hand, sometimes the feeling that you eventually will come to a point of transition can give you the tenacity to persevere the current challenge. But there often seems to be no slackening in distress. Like a rainstorm that will not cease, the waters of discouragement begin to fill the tossing ship with water. Suddenly you experience a sinking feeling. However, there is no way to sink a ship when you do not allow the waters from the outside to get on the inside! If the storms keep coming, the lightning continues to flash, and the thunder thumps on through the night, what matters is keeping the waters out of the inside. Keep that stuff out of your spirit!

Like a desperate sailor trying to plug a leaking ship, Job frantically cast back and forth in his mind, looking for some shred, some fragment of hope, to plug his leaking ship. Exasperated, he sullenly sat in the stupor of his condition and sadly confessed, *"Look, I go forward, but He is not there"* (Job 23:8a). "I can't find Him where I thought He would be." Have you ever told yourself that the storm would be over soon? And the sun came and the sun left, and still the same rains beat vehemently against the ship. It almost feels as if God missed His appointment. You thought He would move by now! Glancing nervously at your watch you think, "Where is He!" Remember, dear friend, God doesn't synchronize His clock by your little mortal watch. He has a set time to bless you; just hold on.

PURPOSE POINT: It actually is satan's trick to make you think help is not coming. That hopelessness then produces anxiety.

TRANSFORMATION MOMENT: The Bible says God's ways are higher than our ways and His thoughts are higher than our thoughts (see Isa. 55:9). He has a plan and purpose for your life. He has a set time to bless you. There will be storms along the way though. Remember the disciples? They were terrified on a boat in the storm and Jesus was sleeping (see Matt. 8:24). Jesus woke up and calmed the storm. He will come through for you too, even if it's not in the way or time you expected.

Don't let the waters of doubt and fear come into your boat. If you are wrestling with fear and doubt, ask Jesus to calm those storms within. Remember what we covered already: you have control over your mind. Focus on who Jesus is, not on the storm.

WHAT IS A PROBLEM IF GOD IS THERE?

And He said, "My Presence will go with you, and I will give you rest."
EXODUS 33:14

S omeone once said that studying the past prepares us for the future. It is important to look backward and see the patterns that cause us to feel some sense of continuity. But Job said, *"Looking back, I could not perceive Him"* (see Job 23:8b). "Why did I have to go through all of this? Is there any reason why I had to have this struggle?" Quite honestly, there are moments when life feels like it has all the purpose of gross insanity. Like a small child cutting paper on the floor, there seems to be no real plan, only actions. These are the times that try men's hearts. These are the times when we seek answers! Sometimes, even more than change, we need answers! "God, if You don't fix it, please, please explain it!" We are reasoning, resourceful creatures. We seek answers. Yet there are times that even after thorough evaluation, we cannot find our way out of the maze of happenstance!

Where is the God who sent an earthquake into the valley of dry bones and put them together? (See Ezekiel 37.) Or where is the God of the clay, who remolds the broken places and mends the jagged edge? (See Isaiah 64:8.) If the truth were told, the God we seek is never far away. The issue is not so much His presence as it is my perception. Many times deliverance doesn't cost God one action. Deliverance comes when my mind accepts His timing and purpose in my life.

In my hours of crises, many times I found myself searching for the place of rest rather than for the answer. If I can find God, I don't need to find money. If I can find God, I don't need to find healing! If I can find Him, my needs become insignificant when I wave them in the light of His presence. What is a problem if God is there? Even in the stench of Job's decaying flesh, he knew that his answer wasn't screaming out for the healing. He was screaming out for the Healer! Do you realize the power of God's presence? I hear many people speak about the acts of God, but have you ever considered the mere presence of God? He doesn't have to do anything but be there, and it is over!

PURPOSE POINT: Many times deliverance doesn't cost God one action. Deliverance comes when my mind accepts His timing and purpose in my life.

TRANSFORMATION MOMENT: No wonder Job was sitting in sackcloth and ashes searching through the rubbish of his life, looking for God. He knew that only the presence of the Lord could bring comfort to his pain! Have you begun your search for a closer manifestation of His grace? Your search alone is worship. When you seek Him, it suggests that you value Him and recognize His ability. The staggering, faulty steps of a seeker are far better than the stance of the complacent. He is not far away. He is in the furnace, moving in the ashes. Look closer. He is never far from the seeker who is on a quest to be in His presence.

God is not far away my friend. If you don't know what He's doing in your life right now, if everything feels confusing, just rest in His presence. And keep on searching.

HE'S WORKING ON THE LEFT HAND

And He said to me, "My grace is sufficient for you,
for My strength is made perfect in weakness."
2 CORINTHIANS 12:9a

Have you been searching and seeking and yet feel that you are getting no closer? Perhaps you are closer than you think. Job told us where to find God. He told where He works. Job said that God works on the left hand! I know you've been looking on the right hand, and I can understand why. The right hand in the Bible symbolizes power and authority. That's why Christ is seated on the right side of God (see Mark 16:19). Whenever you say someone is your right hand, you mean he is next in command or authority. Naturally, then, if you were to search for God, you would look on the right hand. Granted, He is on the right hand. He is full of authority. But you forgot something. His strength is made perfect in weakness (see 2 Cor. 12:9). He displays His glory in the ashes of human frailty. He works on the left hand!

Great growth doesn't come into your life through mountaintop experiences. Great growth comes through the valleys and low places where you feel limited and vulnerable. The time God is really moving in your life may seem to be the lowest moment you have ever experienced. Most believers think that God works when the blessing comes. That's not true! God is working on you, your faith and your character, when the blessing is delayed. The blessing is the reward that comes after you learn obedience through the things you suffered while waiting for it! I wouldn't take any amount of money for the things I learned about God while I was suffering.

Now, I'm not finished suffering, and neither are you! Between every step of faith, between every new dimension of exaltation, there will always be some level of struggle. I am not finished with the left hand—nor do I want to be finished. The prerequisite of the mountain is the valley. If there is no valley, there is no mountain. After you've been through this process a few times, you begin to realize that the valley is only a sign that with a few more steps, you'll be at the mountain again!

PURPOSE POINT: Between every step of faith, between every new dimension of exaltation, there will always be some level of struggle. I am not finished with the left hand—nor do I want to be finished.

TRANSFORMATION MOMENT: I feel by the Holy Spirit that somewhere there is a woman reading whom God wants to make sure this principle gets in her spirit. You have been going through a time of left-side experiences. You've said over and over again, "Where is the move of God that I used to experience? Why am I going through these fiery trials?"

Let me minister to you a minute. God is there with you even now. He is operating in a different realm. He is working with a different hand, but He is still working in your life! In order for Him to do this job in your life, He had to change hands. Trust Him to have the same level of dexterity in His left hand as He does when He moves with the right hand.

WOMAN *Thou Art* BLESSED

JUST HOLD ON!

"Be strong and of good courage, do not fear nor be afraid of them; for the Lord your God, He is the One who goes with you. He will not leave you nor forsake you."

DEUTERONOMY 31:6

There is another issue needing discussion about living on the left side of God. It is difficult to perceive God's workings on the left hand. God makes definite moves on the right hand, but when He works on the left, you may think He has forgotten you! If you've been living on the left side, you've been through a period that didn't seem to have the slightest stirring. It seemed as if everything you wanted to see God move upon, stayed still. "Has He gone on vacation? Has He forgotten His promise?" you've asked. The answer is no! God hasn't forgotten. You simply need to understand that sometimes He moves openly. I call them right-hand blessings. But sometimes He moves silently, tip-toeing around in the invisible, working in the shadows. You can't see Him, for He is working on the left side!

How long does God work on the left? I don't know. It's like the phrase, "Different strokes for different folks." I will tell you one thing, though; Job concluded that God knows the way he takes. That means even when I didn't know where He was, He always knew where I was. God has never taken His eye off you, and He knows where you are every minute. Listen for God's hammering in the spirit. You can't see Him when He's working on the left side; He is invisible over there. It appears that He is not there, but He is.

If the left hand is where He works, and it is; if the left hand is where He teaches us, and it is; then at the end of every class is a promotion. So just hold on!

PURPOSE POINT: God knows the way He takes. That means even when I didn't know where He was, He always knew where I was.

TRANSFORMATION MOMENT: I know so well how hard it is to trust Him when you can't trace Him! But that's exactly what He wants you to do—He wants you to trust Him with either hand. It may seem that everybody is passing you right now. Avoid measuring yourself against other people. God knows when the time is right. His methods may seem crude and His teachings laborious, but His results will be simply breathtaking. Without scams and games, without trickery or politics, God will accomplish a supernatural miracle because you trusted Him while He worked on the left side.

If you feel God is working on the left side in your life, spend time in prayer today committing to trust Him again. Pour out your heart, cry out for help, but commit to hold on. He has never forsaken you, so don't you forsake Him!

YOU SHALL COME FORTH AS PURE GOLD

*The refining pot is for silver and the furnace
for gold, but the Lord tests the hearts.*
PROVERBS 17:3

I've learned to be thankful for the end results. Through every test and trial you must tell yourself what Job said, "I shall come forth as pure gold. I might not come forth today. It might not even be tomorrow. But when God gets through melting out all the impurities and scraping off the dross; when the boiling and the toilings of trouble have receded and the liquified substances in my life have become stable and fixed, then I will shine!" You bubbling, tempestuous saint who is enduring a time of walking through the left side of God, be strong and very courageous. The process always precedes the promise!

Soon you will be reshaped and remade into a gold chalice from which only the King can drink. All dross is discarded; all fear is removed. The spectators will gather to ask how such a wonderful vessel was made out of such poor materials. They will behold the jewels of your testimony and the brilliant glory of that fresh anointing. Some will wonder if you are the same woman that they used to know. How do you answer? Simply stated, just say no!

Now you sit on the Master's right side, ready and available to be used, a vessel of honor unto Him. No matter how glorious it is to sit on His right hand and be brought to a position of power, just remember that although you have overcome now, you were boiled down and hollowed out while you lived on the left side of God. Join me in looking back over your life. Review your left-side experiences. Taste the bitter tears and the cold winds of human indifference and never, ever let anyone make you forget. You and I know. It's our secret, whether we tell them or sit quietly and make small talk. You've not always been where you are or shined as you shine. What can I say? You've come a long way, baby!

🕊 **PURPOSE POINT:** The process always precedes the promise!

🕊 **TRANSFORMATION MOMENT:** Job said, "*When He has tested me...*" (Job 23:10b). The word *when* makes me want to shout because it implies that God has a set time for my going through the test and a set time for bringing me out. Then I'm happy also because it's He who is trying me, not my enemies. It's not the devil, but God! I wouldn't trust anybody else but Him to take me through these left-side experiences. He loves me enough to give me everything I need to live with Him on the left side. To those who have no might He increases strength. New mercies come forth when you fight old problems!

Take some time to look back at those left-hand experiences you've walked through. Can you see how God made you more and more gold, shining and beautiful? Thank Him today for how far you've already come.

BE PROUD OF YOUR DAY OF SMALL BEGINNINGS

For who has despised the day of small things?
For these seven rejoice to see the plumb
line in the hand of Zerubbabel....
ZECHARIAH 4:10

Why do so many people try to convey the image that they have always been on top? The truth is most people have struggled to attain whatever they have. They just try to convince everyone that they have always had it. I, for one, am far more impressed with the wealth of a person's character who doesn't use his success to intimidate others. The real, rich inner stability that comes from gradual success is far more lasting and beneficial than the temperamental theatrics of spiritual yuppies who have never learned their own vulnerabilities. We must not take ourselves too seriously. I believe that God grooms us for greatness in the stockades of struggle.

I remember so well the early struggles that my wife and I had to maintain our family, finances, and overall well-being while building a ministry. I was working a secular job that God wanted me to leave for full-time ministry. Full-time ministry—what a joke! I was scarcely asked to preach any-where that offered more than a few pound cakes, a couple jars of jelly, and if I was lucky, enough gas money to get home. It was there, around old coal stoves in tiny churches that never even considered buying a microphone, that I learned how to preach.

Finally I said yes to full-time ministry because the company I worked for went out of business. I was forced out of my comfort zone into the land of faith. What a frightening experience it was to find myself without everything you could think of: without a job and then a car. Later I was without utilities and often without food. I scraped around doing odd jobs trying to feed two children and a wife without looking like life wasn't working. I am not ashamed to tell you—in fact I am proud to tell you—that I experienced more about God in those desperate days of struggle as I answered the charges of satan with the perseverance of prayer.

PURPOSE POINT: I believe that God grooms us for greatness in the stockades of struggle.

TRANSFORMATION MOMENT: In my day of small beginnings, sometimes I thought God had forgotten me. Often I would preach until sweaty and tired, to rows of empty pews with two or three people. This didn't just last a few months. It was years of my life. I am proud to tell you where I came from. I know I would not be the man I am today without those years persevering through difficul-ties and believing for the promises of God I couldn't see yet.

Character comes through perseverance. You can't persevere without a challenge.

God is not in a rush with you. He has all the time in the world. If you're still in your small beginning, trust that you're right where He wants you. Don't try to rush this season. Wait for His promotion.

THE GIFT OF "GRACE TO ENDURE"

So Satan answered the Lord and said, "Does Job fear
God for nothing? Have You not made a hedge around
him, around his household, and around all that he
has on every side? You have blessed the work of his
hands, and his possessions have increased in the land.
But now, stretch out Your hand and touch all that
he has, and he will surely curse You to Your face!"
JOB 1:9-11

Satan cannot dispute your serving God, but he challenges our reason for serving Him. He says it is for the prominence and protection that God provides. He further insinuates that if things weren't going so well, we would not praise God so fervently. The devil is a liar! In each of our lives, in one way or another, we will face times when we must answer satan's charges and prove that even in the storm, He is still God!

My early years of challenge sorely tried all that was in me. My pride, my self-esteem, and my self-confidence teetered like a child learning to ride a bicycle. My greatest fear was that it would never end. I feared that, like a person stuck in an elevator, I would spend the rest of my life between floors—neither here nor there in an intermediate stage of transition. I felt like a shoulder out of joint and in pain. I learned, however, that if you can remember your beginnings and still reach toward your goals, God will bless you with things without fear of those items becoming idols in your life.

There is a strange sense of competence that comes from being born in the flames of struggle. How wildly exuberant are the first steps of the child who earlier was mobile only through crawling on his hands and knees. Often we don't realize how severe our beginnings were until we are out or about to come out of them. Then the grace lifts and we behold the utter devastating truth about what we just came through. But, oddly, there is a glory in the agonizing of early years that people who didn't have to struggle seem not to possess.

PURPOSE POINT: Often we don't realize how severe our beginnings were until we are out or about to come out of them.

TRANSFORMATION MOMENT: When you are in those small beginnings, it can feel like it will never end. As I said, that was my biggest fear. The concern over the future coupled with the fear of failure brings us to the posture of prayer. I don't think I completely realized how severe my early years were because I saw them through the tinted glasses of grace. I had been gifted with the grace to endure. What a gift to look back and see He never once left my side. What a gift to be purified in God's fire and endure. I can't say it enough, God has a purpose for your life. He will bless you...in His time.

Do you have the grace to endure, beloved? Ask God to show you His perspective on your small beginnings, whether they are in the past or the present.

GOD, THE MASTER BUILDER, EMPHASIZES FOUNDATIONS

According to the grace of God which was given to me,
as a wise master builder I have laid the foundation, and
another builds on it. But let each one take heed how
he builds on it. For no other foundation can anyone
lay than that which is laid, which is Jesus Christ.

1 CORINTHIANS 3:10-11

I have found God to be a builder of men and women. When He builds, He emphasizes the foundation. A foundation, once it is laid, is neither visible nor attractive, but nevertheless still quite necessary. When God begins to establish the foundation, He does it in the feeble, frail beginnings of our lives. God is the Master Builder. He knows what kind of beginning we need and He lays His foundation in the struggles of our formative years.

Many misunderstand the prophecies of the Lord and so feel discontentment and despair. Just because God promises to move in your life and anoints you to do a particular function doesn't mean that your foundation will be immediately built. Joseph received a dream from the Lord that showed him ruling and reigning over his brothers, but in the next event his brothers stripped him, beat him, and tossed him in a hole. Can you imagine what the devil said to Joseph while he nursed his scrapes and bruises in the dark hole of small beginnings?

Swallowed up with bruises and scars, he listened to the sound of depression sweeping through his throbbing head that beat like the congo drums of an African warrior. Satan's laugh filled the dark channels of the hole with his evil hysteria. "So you were going to reign, were you? I thought the dream said you were in charge," the enemy taunted. Satan didn't understand that all great prophecies start out small. Like chestnuts in the hand of a child, those same chestnuts will one day be large enough to hold a child like the one who once held them. God's methods may seem crude, but His purpose is to provide wonderful success. Don't die in the hole! God hasn't changed His mind. He is a Master Builder and He spends extra time laying a great foundation.

PURPOSE POINT: All great prophecies start out small. Like chestnuts in the hand of a child, those same chestnuts will one day be large enough to hold a child like the one who once held them.

TRANSFORMATION MOMENT: Maybe you have big dreams or prophetic words that seem a long way off. If it seems like you've been in a long, hidden season of small beginnings, you are in very good company. Directly after David was anointed to lead Israel, he was sent back into the field to feed the sheep. In those lonely fields, David killed lions and bears with no one watching. He worshiped God in those still, silent nights. It was there where he became the brave man who killed Goliath. It was there God developed his heart and his character to become a king.

Take time to remember the dreams and prophetic words over your life today, dear daughter. No matter what today looks like, keep those words close to your heart and keep believing! God has not changed His mind about you.

Day Sixty-Three

INSTANT SUCCESS IS NOT GOD'S WAY

And the Scripture was fulfilled which says, "Abraham believed God, and it was accounted to him for righteousness." And he was called the friend of God.
JAMES 2:23

I am afraid that too many Christians pop off the altar like cardboard instant waffles out of the freezer. They are overnight wonders. They are 24-hour pastors with a Bible they haven't read and a briefcase more valuable than the sermons in it! I know this sounds old-fashioned, but I believe anything worth doing is worth doing well. God Himself takes His time developing us. No instant success will do. He wants to put the quality in before the name goes out.

A small beginning is just the prelude to a tremendous crescendo at the finale! Many of God's masterpieces were developed in small obscure circumstances. Moses, the messiah of the Old Testament sent to the lost sheep of Israel, was trained in leadership while shoveling sheep dung on the backside of the desert. There was no fancy finishing school for this boy. Granted, his discipline was developed in the royal courts of Pharaoh's house, but his disposition was shaped through

181

a failure in his life and a desert kingdom with no one to lead but flies, gnats, and sheep. Who would have thought, looking at Moses' church of goat deacons and gnats for choir members, that he later would lead the greatest movement in the history of Old Testament theology?

Who would have guessed that old impotent Abraham, whose sun had gone down and force gone out, would finally father a nation—in fact, a nationality? Sarah laughed when she heard the word that she would have a child; she was already well past child-bearing age (see Gen. 18:12). But God! Their promise was fulfilled well beyond their expectations. You can't tell what's in you by looking at you. God is establishing patience, character, and concentration in the school of "nothing seems to be happening." Take the class and get the course credit; it's working for your good.

🐦 **PURPOSE POINT:** You can't tell what's in you by looking at you. God is establishing patience, character, and concentration in the school of "nothing seems to be happening."

🐦 **TRANSFORMATION MOMENT:** Are you chasing instant success? Are you willing to go through God's training school even if it takes longer than you hoped for? Throughout the Bible, you can read story after story of men and women formed in the fires of trials. The long, hidden years were the very place where they dug deep wells of faith and where God built firm foundations in them. Sometimes we think we've done something wrong if "nothing is happening." The reality is we just need to recognize God's methods of building great men and women. Relationship with Him is the best part of the journey.

What if the goal is not what you do for God but what He is doing within you? Are you willing to surrender your timing to Him?

WOE UNTO THE WOMAN WHOSE MINISTRY BECOMES BIGGER THAN SHE IS!

For unto us a Child is born, unto us a Son is given;
and the government will be upon His shoulder. And
His name will be called Wonderful, Counselor,
Mighty God, Everlasting Father, Prince of Peace.
ISAIAH 9:6

When the first man Adam was created, he was created full grown. He had no childhood, no small things. He was just immediately a man. But when it was time for the last man Adam, God didn't create Him full grown. No, He took His time and laid a foundation. He was born a child and laid in a manger. The Manager of the universe was laid in a manger. The Bible says that He grew in favor with God and man (see Luke 2:52). Not too fast, but He grew. Please allow yourself time to grow.

Once I was praying for the Lord to move mightily in my ministry. I had asked, fasted, and prayed. I had probably begged a little and foamed at the mouth too, but none of it hurried the plan of God in my life. After many days of absolute silence, He finally sent me a little answer. The Lord answered my prayer by saying, "You are concerned about building a ministry, but I am concerned about building a man." He concluded by mentioning this warning, which has echoed in my ears all of my life. He said, "Woe unto the man whose ministry becomes bigger than he is!" Since then I have concerned myself with praying for the minister and not for the ministry. I realized that if the house outgrows the foundation, gradually the foundation will crack, the walls will collapse, and great will be the fall of it!

I am still amazed at who I am becoming as I put my life daily into His hands. He is changing me. He's not finished. There is so much more that needs to be done. Every day I see more immaturity in me. But, what a sharp contrast I am now to what I was.

PURPOSE POINT: The Lord answered my prayer by saying, "You are concerned about building a ministry, but I am concerned about building a man."

TRANSFORMATION MOMENT: No matter what you are trying to build, whether it is a business, a ministry, or a relationship, give it time to grow. Some of the best friendships start out gradually. Some of the strongest Christians once desperately needed prayer for their weaknesses and thought things would never change. When I was concerned over the speed of my progress and fervently praying for my ministry to grow, it was God's voice that changed everything. His words completely shifted my prayers from the ministry to the minister.

Ask God to speak directly to your heart about what He is doing in your season and let that bring the peace. Don't rush the firm foundation.

WOMAN *Thou Art* BLESSED

THANK GOD FOR YOUR SMALL BEGINNINGS

*And do not be called teachers; for One is your
Teacher, the Christ. But he who is greatest
among you shall be your servant.*
MATTHEW 23:10-11

Humility is a necessity when you know that every accomplishment had to be the result of the wise Master Builder who knows when to do what. He knew when I needed friends. He knew when I needed to sit silently in the night, wrap my arms around my limitations, and whisper a soft request for help into the abyss of my pain. He is the One who rolls back the clouds on the storms and orders the rain to stop. Oh, how I trust Him more dearly and more nearly than I have ever trusted Him before. He is too wise to make a mistake!

What a joy it is to be at peace with who you are and where you are in your life. How restful it is to not try and beat the clock with friends or try to prove anything to foes. You will never change their minds anyway, so change your own. I want to be better—to have a better character, better confidence, and a better attitude! The desire to be bigger will not allow you to rest, relax, or enjoy your blessing. The desire to be better, however, will afford you a barefoot stroll down a deserted beach. You can sit in the sand, throw shells into the water, and shiver when the tide rushes up too high. Sing into the wind a song out of tune. It may not harmonize, but it will be full of therapy. There are probably many things you didn't get done and so much you have left to do. But isn't it nice to sigh, relax, and just thank God for the things—the little, tiny, small things—that you know He brought you through. Thank God for small things.

PURPOSE POINT: What a joy it is to be at peace with who you are and where you are in your life. How restful it is to not try and beat the clock with friends or try to prove anything to foes.

TRANSFORMATION MOMENT: If you are praying, "Lord, make me bigger," you are probably miserable, although prayerful. Did you know you can be prayerful and still be miserable? Anytime you use prayer to change God, who is perfect, instead of using prayer to change yourself, you are miserable. Stop manipulating God! Stop trying to learn something you can say to God to make Him do what He knows you are not ready to endure or receive. Instead, try praying this: "Lord, make me better." I admit that better is harder to measure and not as noticeable to the eye. But better will overcome bigger every time. Remember, the greatest in the Kingdom is the servant of all.

I really mean it, pray that God will make you better. Pray that God will build a deep foundation and a solid character in you.

YOU CAN'T CHANGE THE PRICE TAGS

If anyone's work which he has built on it
endures, he will receive a reward.
1 CORINTHIANS 3:14

Many people want to be successful, but not everyone realizes that success is given only at the end of great struggle. If it were easy, anybody could do it. Success is the reward that God gives to the diligent who, through perseverance, obtain the promise. There is no way to receive what God has for your life without fighting the obstacles and challenges that block your way to conquest. In fact, people who procrastinate do so because they are desperately trying to find a way to reach the goal without going through the struggle.

When I was a youngster, we kids used to change the price tags on the items we could not afford. We weren't stealing, we thought, because we did pay something, just not the real price. Many people are trying to do the same thing today in their spiritual life. They're attempting to get a discount on the promises of God. That doesn't work in the Kingdom. Whatever it costs, it costs; there's no swapping the price tags.

You must pay your own way. Your payment helps you to appreciate the blessings when they come because you know the expense. You will not easily jeopardize the welfare of something not easily attained. The zeal it takes to be effective at accomplishing a goal ushers you up the steps of life.

Successful people tend to be passionate people who have intense desire. I admit there are many passionate people who are not successful. But if you can focus passion for a divine purpose, you will be successful. Some people never use their desire in a positive way. Instead of harnessing it and allowing it to become the force they use to overcome hindrances, it becomes a source of frustration and cynicism. Success only comes to a person who is committed to a cause or has a passion to achieve. It takes more than a mere whimsical musing over a speculative end. It takes floor-walking, devil-stomping, anointed tenacity to overcome the limitations that are always surrounding what you want to do for your God, yourself, and your family!

PURPOSE POINT: You will not easily jeopardize the welfare of something not easily attained. The zeal it takes to be effective at accomplishing a goal ushers you up the steps of life.

TRANSFORMATION MOMENT: If you don't have sufficient passion, you will never have the force to overcome limitations and satanic restrictions. Power emerges from the heart of a woman who is relentlessly driven toward a goal. Desire is kindled in the furnace of need—an unfulfilled need.

WOMAN *Thou Art* BLESSED

It is a need that refuses to be placated and a need that will not be silent. Many people who set out to accomplish goals are so easily discouraged or intimidated by their own anxieties that they relinquish their right to fight for their dreams. However, if there is a tenacious burning desire in the pit of your stomach, you become very difficult to discourage.

The crux of the matter basically is this: "How bad do you want to be blessed?" How strong is your desire for accomplishment in your life? Think and pray into this today.

DON'T LET JEALOUSY DERAIL YOU

So the Lord said to Cain, "Why are you angry?
And why has your countenance fallen? If you
do well, will you not be accepted? And if you do
not do well, sin lies at the door. And its desire
is for you, but you should rule over it."
GENESIS 4:6-7

It is amazing the relationships that can be lost as you travel upward. As you journey up the steps to purpose, it becomes increasingly difficult to be successful without others finding you offensive. Some people will find your success offensive, whether or not you are arrogant. They are offended at what God does for you. I call those people "Cain's children." They will murder you because you have God's favor. Watch out for them. They will not rejoice with you. They can't be glad for you because somehow they feel your success came at their expense. They foolishly believe that you have their blessing. No diplomacy can calm a jealous heart. They don't want to pay what you paid, but they want to have what you have.

Cain's children will invite you into their field to destroy you. Must you then be defensive? How can you defend yourself from another person's reaction to you? Then you become imprisoned by paranoia. It is difficult to be careful without being distrustful and cynical. "Are we not brothers and sisters?" Sure we are. Yet Jesus said, *"and a man's enemies will be those of his own household."* (Matt. 10:36). Your enemy will not wound you because he is too far way. In order to be a good Judas, he or she must be at the table with the victim of his betrayal! Who sits at your table?

Imagine Jesus, at the height of His ministerial career, sitting at the table with John, the beloved, on one side and Judas, the betrayer, on the other. The problem is in discerning which one is which. One of them is close enough to lay his head on your breast. The other has enough access to you to betray you with a kiss. They are both intimate, but one is lethal. Yet, in the midst of this harsh and rather bleak panoramic view of success, you must depend on the Lord to keep whatever He commits into your hands, at least until His purpose is accomplished. Keep your affections on the Giver and not the gifts. "Lord, help us to keep our eyes on the things that will not change."

PURPOSE POINT: As you journey up the steps to purpose, it becomes increasingly difficult to be successful without others finding you offensive.

TRANSFORMATION MOMENT: As long as you're in the day of small beginnings, you're acceptable. People don't always want to see you move on—especially if they perceive you as moving more rapidly than they are. Or receiving more favor and blessing. As painful as it is to be criticized by those you are in covenant with, it's far worse to give up the course that God has for you just for their acceptance. As you need to be affirmed and understood, at some point you must ask yourself, "How much am I willing to lose in order to be accepted?" Don't let this scare you or make you defensive. Instead, keep your eyes fixed on God and fellowship with the true friends like John.

Daughter, if you are facing criticism and ridicule, don't let it get you off course. Surrender these comments and judgements back to God and forgive those who have not celebrated you.

COUNT THE COST TO BE BLESSED

His lord said to him, "Well done, good and faithful servant; you have been faithful over a few things, I will make you ruler over many things. Enter into the joy of your lord."

MATTHEW 25:23

Another consideration with success is this: the more you have or own, the more you are responsible for. People who have no car need no gas. With every blessing there is an additional responsibility. How many times have you prayed for a blessing? Then, when you received it, you realized there were strings attached that you didn't originally consider? To be honest, being blessed is hard work. Everything God gives you requires maintenance. God gave Adam and Eve the Garden, but they still had to dress it. There is a "down" side to every blessing. That is why Jesus said, *"No man builds without counting the cost"* (see Luke 14:28-30). You must ask yourself if you are willing to pay the price to get the blessing.

With these questions we have already weeded out half the people who say they want something from the Lord. We have weeded out all the women who say they want a husband and children but don't want to cook, care, or clean. We have weeded out all the men who say they want a wife but don't want to love, provide, and nourish! Most people are in love with the image of success, but they haven't contemplated the reality of possessing the blessing. It is a good thing God doesn't give us everything we ask for because we want some things simply because they look good in someone else's life. The truth is, we are not ready for those things and it would probably kill us to receive what we are not prepared to maintain.

I believe that God starts His children out with what they have to teach consistency on the level they are on. There must be an inner growth in your ability to withstand the struggles that accompany the things you have. I am so glad that God allowed me to go through the pain-ridden days of stress and rejection early in my life. I found out that if you really want to pursue your dream, there is a place in God whereby you build up an immunity to the adversity of success. It is simply a matter of survival.

🐦 **PURPOSE POINT:** There must be an inner growth in your ability to withstand the struggles that accompany the things you have.

🐦 **TRANSFORMATION MOMENT:** Daughter, if you are always weeping over rejection and misunderstanding, if you're always upset over who doesn't accept you into their circles anymore, you may be suffering from an immunity deficiency syndrome. You waste precious time of communion when you ask God to change the minds of people. It is not the people or the pressure that must change, it is you. In order to survive the stresses of success, you must build up an immunity to those things that won't change. Thank God that He provides elasticity for us. Remember, you can't switch price tags just because you don't like the price.

My constant prayer is, "Lord, change me until this doesn't hurt anymore." Pray that with me today.

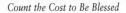

STIR THE EMBERS AND IGNITE YOUR PASSION

Therefore I remind you to stir up the gift of God
which is in you through the laying on of my hands.
2 TIMOTHY 1:6

Having pastored in the coal fields of West Virginia, I know about wood and coal stoves. You can bank the fire by placing ashes all around it. Then it will not burn out as rapidly and will last through the night. In the frosty chill of the morning you do not need to rebuild the fire, for beneath the ashes lay crimson embers waiting to be stirred. These embers explode into a fire when they are stirred correctly. Many people have gone through situations that banked their fire. The fire isn't dead, but its burning is not as brilliant as it once was. I am glad that if you have an inner desire to survive or succeed, then you only need a stirring for the embers of passion to ignite in your life.

I love to surround myself with people who can stir up the fire in me. Some people in the Body of Christ know just what to say to ignite the very fire in you. However, no one can ignite in you what you do not possess! If the cold winds of opposition have banked the fire and your dream is dying down, I challenge you to rekindle your desire to achieve whatever God has called you to do. Don't lose your fire. You need that continued spark for excellence to overcome all the blight of being ostracized.

Fire manifests itself in two ways. First, it gives light. Whenever you maintain your fire, it produces the light of optimism against the blackness of crises and critics alike. As long as you maintain that fire-like attitude, you will find a way to survive the struggle. A person never dies with a twinkle in his eyes. Second, fire gives heat. Heat can't be seen, but it can be felt. When you are burning with the passion to survive, the heat can be felt. Invisible but effective, your intensity is always detected in your speech and attitude.

PURPOSE POINT: I love to surround myself with people who can stir up the fire in me.

TRANSFORMATION MOMENT: Every man and woman of God must also remember that fire needs fuel. Feed the fire. Feed it with the words of people who motivate you. Feed it with vision and purpose. When stress comes, fan the flames. Gather the wood. Pour gasoline if you have to, but don't let it die! How many cold nights I have warmed my cold feet by the fires of my innermost desire to complete a goal for my life. No one knows how hot the embers glow beneath the ashes of adversity.

Is your fire blazing or has it died down to embers? Ask the Holy Spirit to show you how to fan the flames. Especially ask Him to highlight other people that stir up the fire. Focus on those friendships as you press on toward your goals.

DIG FOR YOUR OWN GOLD

For as the body is one and has many members,
but all the members of that one body, being
many, are one body, so also is Christ.
1 CORINTHIANS 12:12

Sometimes just seeing God bless someone else gives you the fortitude to put a demand on the promise that God has given you. I don't mean envy, but a strong provocation to receive. I have learned how to rejoice over the blessings of my brother and realize that the same God who blessed him can bless me also. If seeing others blessed makes you want to sabotage their success, then you will not be fruitful. Other people's blessings ought to challenge you to see that it can be done. Don't begrudge other people's blessings, simply ask for your own.

Success cannot be defined in generalities; it can be defined only according to individual purpose and divine direction. If you don't understand this concept, you can have great riches or fame and still be unsuccessful. You would be surprised at how many highly anointed people are tormented by a need to evaluate themselves in the light of another's calling. Your assignment is to dig for your own gold. Just cultivate what the

Lord has given to you. It's simple: Find out what you have to work with, and then work it, work it, work it!

I am always concerned that Christians not manipulate each other by trying to get people to worship their talents rather than God's purpose for their lives. How can any person know you well enough to discern whether you are successful, other than the God who created you? In short, there is no way to define success without examining purpose. What did the inventor have in mind when he made the machine? That is the first question. The second question asks, "Did it accomplish the purpose it was created to perform?" It doesn't matter what else it did; if it didn't satisfy the mandate of its creator, it is unsuccessful. When people other than the Creator define success, it becomes idolatry. Some people would have you worship at the shrine of their accomplishments. Of course you should appreciate and encourage them, but don't be manipulated by them.

PURPOSE POINT: Success cannot be defined in generalities; it can be defined only according to individual purpose and divine direction.

TRANSFORMATION MOMENT: Suppose your heart told your kidneys, "Unless you pump blood, you are not successful." Never mind that the kidneys purify the blood that the heart pumps. It would be foolish for the kidneys to believe that statement. It would shut down the whole body! That's what happens when we, as the Body, fail to maintain our individuality! We are a body with many parts and many purposes. That's why godly success can only be defined in light of your divine purpose.

Do you tend to compare yourself with others or measure your success against theirs? Ask the Holy Spirit to show you where your gold is and to reshape your idea of success based on His design for you.

IF YOU WANT IT, PAY THE PRICE

...For everyone to whom much is given, from him much will be required; and to whom much has been committed, of him they will ask the more.
LUKE 12:48

Not everyone can handle success. Some may choose tranquility over notoriety. They don't like criticism and they abhor pressure. But if you are the kind of woman who desperately needs to attain the hope of her calling, then go for it. Some people will never be satisfied with sitting on the bench cheering for others who paid the price to play the game. Locked within them is an inner ambitious intrigue not predicated on jealousy or intimidation. It is built upon an inner need to unlock a predestined purpose. For them, it does not matter. Inflationary times may escalate the price of their dreams, but whatever the price, they are compelled, drawn, and almost driven toward a hope.

Many people are drawn toward their destiny with such a force and an attraction that regardless of what it takes, what they must readjust, or what they must discipline, they simply must respond to life's challenges. Neither lethal nor dangerous, they merely move aggressively toward purpose. For myself, I am not afraid of dying; I am not afraid of leaving as much as I am afraid of not living first. What absolutely terrifies me is the thought that I would stand beside life like a miser who longs for a certain article but is too crippled by his incessant fear of expense to buy. If you want it, pay the price.

I confess, I have cried huge salty tears. I have felt the bitter pangs of rejection and criticism. I admit there were times that I rocked my worries to sleep in the middle of the night. Know all this and understand that I have not yet seen a day that made me regret the decision to run my course.

PURPOSE POINT: For myself, I am not afraid of dying; I am not afraid of leaving as much as I am afraid of not living first.

TRANSFORMATION MOMENT: How far or how fast you run in comparison with others doesn't matter. Whether you win trophies or receive great accolades doesn't matter. What matters is that you stretch your legs and run in the wind. It is only your shadow that you run against. It is your own destiny that you stride beside. Don't let fear stop you. Don't let other people push you down. Run your race as the powerful woman of God you really are. Live without regret. Be a woman of purpose.

What is your biggest fear? Are you more afraid of dying or of not fully living? Ask God to show you any fears or obstacles standing in the way of your race. Partner with Him to remove every hinderance and run your race.

Day Seventy-Two

GO FOR BROKE THROUGH THE FINISH LINE!

Therefore we also, since we are surrounded by so great a cloud of witnesses, let us lay aside every weight, and the sin which so easily ensnares us, and let us run with endurance the race that is set before us.

HEBREWS 12:1

I am told that distance runners make long, steady strides and that their emphasis is on endurance, not speed. They take their laps and stretch their limitations, giving themselves over to committing their strength to a goal. Turning corners with agility, running shoes banging the pavement, heads high, backs straight—they are in pursuit of a goal. I am told that as they near the finish line, there is a final burst of energy that kicks in like the final cylinders in an engine. It is the last lap; there are no excuses; it's now or never. Now they go for broke!

At least once, before they roll you in on a slab and put a name tag on your cold stiff toe, you owe it to your God and to yourself to experience in some area in your life that last-lap feeling of giving your all. I want to warn you, though, that it hurts to push yourself. It is not easy to get up early every

205

morning while others sleep and prepare for the challenge. Like Jesus in the garden of Gethsemane, it is difficult to find someone who will stand with you while you are in preparation. But there can be no celebration without preparation.

The question is universal but the answer is totally individual. Can *you* stand to be blessed? If you answer yes, then I want to tell you this: The only way to be blessed is to stand! When you can't seem to put one foot in front of the other, stand. When days come that challenge your destiny, just stand. Realize that there has never been a day that lasted forever. You can't afford to crumple onto your knees like a weak, whimpering lily blown over by a windstorm. Bite your lip, taste your tears, but stand on what God showed you in the night until it happens in the light.

PURPOSE POINT: The only way to be blessed is to stand! When you can't seem to put one foot in front of the other, stand. When days come that challenge your destiny, just stand.

TRANSFORMATION MOMENT: If after you calculate the rejection, controversy, criticism, and isolation, you still want it, then realize that you cannot stand the pain of a cross unless you have before you something more important than the pain you endure in the process. Your purpose is worth any cost. Do not stop short of the finish line. Give all that is in you to run your course. Remember, you are not running alone, daughter. A great cloud of witnesses is cheering you on (see Heb. 12:1). Look to Jesus, the Author and the Finisher of your faith (see Heb. 12:2). Build the endurance of faith and the muscles of perseverance so you will also get the gold.

What did God show you in the night? Call to mind the things you're running toward, the promises of God for you personally. Let them fuel you to keep running today.

THE PRIZE BEYOND THE FINISH LINE

*Do you not know that those who run in a
race all run, but one receives the prize? Run
in such a way that you may obtain it.*

1 CORINTHIANS 9:24

As you're running your race on this earth, there must be something beyond the acquisition of a goal. Many people spend all their lives trying to attain a goal. When they finally achieve it, they still secretly feel empty and unfulfilled. This will happen even in the pursuit of godly goals and successes if we don't reach beyond the mere accomplishment of an ambitious pursuit. In short, success doesn't save! Why then does God put the desire to attain in the hearts of His men and women if He knows that at the end is, as Solomon so aptly put it, *"Vanity of vanities...all is vanity"* (Eccles. 12:8)? Could it be that we who have achieved something of effectiveness must then reach a turn in the road and begin to worship God beyond the goal!

A runner trains himself to achieve a goal. That goal ultimately is to break the ribbon, the mark of success. After he has broken the ribbon, if there is no prize beyond the goal, then the race seems in vain. No runner would run a race and then receive the broken ribbon as the symbol of his success. At the end of the race is a prize unrelated to the race itself—a trophy that can be given only to people who have reached the pinnacle of accomplishment. What we must understand in the back of our minds as we ascend toward God's purpose is it blesses God when we attain what we were created to attain. It is His eternal purpose that we pursue. However, we can be blessed only by the God behind the purpose. If we build a great cathedral for the Lord and fail to touch the God whom the cathedral is for, what good is the building aside from God?

PURPOSE POINT: Could it be that we who have achieved something of effectiveness must then reach a turn in the road and begin to worship God beyond the goal!

TRANSFORMATION MOMENT: There is a prize beyond the finish line. When we build in this world, there is actually an eternal Kingdom work being done in our lives. God is with us and for us, and as we achieve our unique purpose, His eternal Kingdom comes. If we build in our own strength for our own glory, there is no divine purpose. That's when we feel like Solomon, empty at the end. Even the greatest achievements won't satisfy you without God's presence. But when you see God holding a giant trophy, standing at the end of your race, you can't help but praise Him. He created us to achieve and to build, but it must be unto His glory and for His purpose in our lives.

What are you building right now? Do you see the eternal purposes of God behind your efforts?

YOU NEED PRESENCE AND PURPOSE

Also I heard the voice of the Lord, saying:
"Whom shall I send, and who will go for Us?"
Then I said, "Here am I! Send me."
ISAIAH 6:8

Why are we always such extremists? Some of us spend all our lives doing absolutely nothing for the Lord. We are constantly in His presence, praising His name, but we fail to accomplish anything relative to His purpose. Isaiah was in the presence of God to such a degree that the glory of the Lord filled the temple like a train, and the doorpost moved (see Isa. 6:1-4). Nevertheless, there was still a time when God sent him from His presence to accomplish His purpose. As an eagle stirs her nest, so God must challenge us to leave the familiar places and perform the uncertain future of putting into practice the total of all we have learned in the Lord's presence. The priest went into the Holy of Holies to see the glory of the Lord, but the work of the Lord was to be performed outside the veiled place of secret consecration. As Isaiah said, *"Here am I; send me"* (Isa. 6:8), go from the gluttony of storing up the treasure to being a vessel God can use!

The other extreme is equally, if not more, dangerous. What makes us think we can do the work of the Lord and never spend time with the Lord of the work? We get burned out when we do not keep fresh fire burning within! We need the kind of fire that comes from putting down all the work and saying to the Lord, "I need my time with You." What good is it to break the finish line if you do not go beyond that temporary moment of self-aggrandizement to receive a valued reward? The accomplishment isn't reward enough because once it is attained, it ceases to be alluring.

🐦 **PURPOSE POINT:** As an eagle stirs her nest, so God must challenge us to leave the familiar places and perform the uncertain future of putting into practice the total of all we have learned in the Lord's presence.

🐦 **TRANSFORMATION MOMENT:** In this context, it is not all or nothing, it is both and more. God's presence is the cocoon where we receive identity and purpose. Full joy and abundant life are in Him. Then it is time to fly, it's time to build. Like that loving eagle, Father God will kick you out of the nest. He wants to see you fly because He knows you can and because He knows how glorious it will be. On the other hand, if you fly on your own strength and fail to catch the wind of His presence, you'll become exhausted. We are created to soar with God. That's where your strength comes from.

Do you find yourself on one of these extremes? Ask God to kick you out of the nest or ask God to catch you up again in the wind of His presence.

ONLY HE CAN SATISFY

*And everyone who competes for the prize is temperate
in all things. Now they do it to obtain a perishable
crown, but we for an imperishable crown.*

1 CORINTHIANS 9:25

After we reach a goal, we do not continue to celebrate what we have already accomplished. Since the beauty of the moment soon fades and you find yourself again seeking new conquest, there must be something beyond just achieving goals and setting new goals. You would be surprised at the number of pastors and leaders all across this country who race wildly from one goal to the other without ever feeling fulfilled by their accomplishments. What is even worse is the fact that other men and women often envy and sometimes hate these ministers because they would love to have what these ministers have attained. Yet these dear ones themselves can't see their own worth. Little does anyone know that these spiritual celebrities are being widely driven by the need to accomplish without ever being fulfilled. It is the cruelest form of torture to be secretly dying of the success which others envy.

Release comes so you can enter the presence of God to be restored. To be restored means to be built back up, to be restocked. Only God can put back into you what striving took out. Will you strive for a goal again? Yes! You need to strive, but you don't need the obsession that it can create. There will never be anything that God gives you to do that will replace what God's mere presence will give. You will never build your self-esteem by accomplishing goals because, as in the case of my twins, once you've done it, it's done! No lasting affirmation comes from a mountain that has been climbed. Only Christ can save you, affirm you, and speak to how you feel about yourself.

PURPOSE POINT: There will never be anything that God gives you to do that will replace what God's mere presence will give.

TRANSFORMATION MOMENT: The praises of men and women will fall into the abyss of a leaky heart. When you have a crack, everything in you will leak out. Let God fix it. Your job can't do it. Marriage can't do it. Children can't do it. Another graduate degree can't do it, but God can! He is the Doctor who specialized in reconstructive surgery! His presence is where you are renewed and refreshed. It's where you hear His voice speaking truth that transforms everything. You can't just run from one thing to the next, never taking time to breath Him in and be filled by His love for you.

This morning, don't rush to the next thing. Take some time to linger in His presence. Ask Him to fill every empty place in your heart. Let this transformation work continue in your heart. And remember the beautiful, colorful butterfly you are becoming!

THE INNER RINGING

*The twenty-four elders fall down before Him who
sits on the throne and worship Him who lives forever
and ever, and cast their crowns before the throne,
saying: "You are worthy, O Lord, to receive glory
and honor and power; for You created all things,
and by Your will they exist and were created."*

REVELATION 4:10-11

There is a place in the presence of God where crowns
lose their luster. There is a place where the accolades
of men sound brash and out of pitch. There is a place where
all our memorials of great accomplishments seem like dusty
stones gathered by bored children who had nothing better
to collect. There are times when we trade success for solace.
In Revelation, 24 elders traded their golden, jewel-encrusted
crowns for a tear-stained moment in the presence of a blood-
stained Lamb. Many wonderful people are suffering with
their success because they cannot discern when to throw
down their crowns and just worship.

We as Christians reach fulfillment when we come to the
point where we bring to the Lord all that we have and worship Him on the other side of accomplishment. This need to
return an answer to the Sender is as instinctive as answering a

ringing telephone. There is a ringing in the heart of a believer that requires an answer. Why do we answer a phone? We do so because of our insatiable curiosity to know who is calling. He is calling us. His ring has sounded through our triumphs and conquests. A deep sound in the recesses of a heart turned toward God suggests that there is a deeper relationship on the other side of the blessing. As wonderful as it is to be blessed with promises, there is still a faint ringing that suggests the Blesser is better than the blessing. It is a ringing that many people overlook. The noise of the bustling, blaring sound of survival can be deafening. There must be a degree of spirituality in order to hear and respond to the inner ringing of the call of God!

PURPOSE POINT: A deep sound in the recesses of a heart turned toward God suggests that there is a deeper relationship on the other side of the blessing.

TRANSFORMATION MOMENT: When you come into the presence of God and His anointing, cast down your crowns and bend your knees. You can let it go and still not lose it. Like the 24 elders in Revelation, you must learn to trade a monument for a moment. The real reward you need to seek can be paid only by the one who hired you—God Himself. You see, the 24 elders knew that they had received results and rewards, but the real credit went to the Lord. They were wise enough not to be too impressed with their own success. They knew that it was God all the time. When you learn to give the glory back to God, you will be fulfilled in His presence and not frustrated by worshiping His presents!

Will you take a moment to enter His presence in worship today? Lay your crowns at His feet and look upon His beautiful face.

NO MATTER HOW FAR GOD TAKES YOU, DON'T LOSE YOUR BALANCE

Therefore humble yourselves under the mighty hand of God, that He may exalt you in due time.
1 PETER 5:6

I have a question I would like you to ponder. What makes a connoisseur of fine restaurants leave the elegant, aristocratic atmospheres and the succulent cuisine of gourmet food, only to stop by a hamburger joint for a sandwich and fries? Time's up. Here's the answer. Each of us has within us a need for balance and a sense of normalcy. It is so important that we balance our areas of expertise with plain everyday humanism. I started out preaching in the most adverse of circumstances. I don't think I really knew how adverse they were because I had nothing to compare them to. I went from sleeping in a child's bedroom of somebody's home to penthouse suites. I remember ministering in churches where the finances did not allow for a hotel room or even a real guest room. The evangelist would stay with the pastor, and usually the pastor had a house full of children. One of these bright-eyed children would have to give up his or her room to accommodate the man of God. I still pray for those families who gave what they had to make me as comfortable as they could. I earnestly appreciate it.

Imagine me, nearly six-foot-three-inches tall and the better part of 280 pounds, sleeping in a canopied bed designed for a ten-year-old girl with ribbons in her hair. I still break out into hysterical laughter as I picture myself sticking one extremity after the other out of the bed, trying to find a place to sleep! Now, I normally have excellent accommodations. God has blessed me to be able to minister in settings that can better accommodate the needs I have and support my family, which is a great blessing. In spite of all this improvement, on occasion I still seek to leave the well-insulated environment of a first-class establishment. I'll go find a little, "do drop in" kind of a place and then return to my suite with some down-home food and probably more grease than I could jog off in a year!

Balance helps to keep you from falling. It does not guarantee that you won't fall, but it does safeguard against the possibility. Never lose your balance—it will assist you in being a person and not just a personality.

🐦 **PURPOSE POINT:** Balance helps to keep you from falling. It does not guarantee that you won't fall, but it does safeguard against the possibility.

🐦 **TRANSFORMATION MOMENT:** I believe that people need to see that God uses, as my friend Danniebelle wrote, "Ordinary People." If that weren't true, who would He use? Ordinary people who have extraordinary callings are the order of the day in this age. You will see in this age God raising Davids to the forefront, not Sauls. He will raise up men and women who don't look as if they would be kings. When you get your crown, don't use it to belittle people who need you. Instead cast it at the feet of the Lord who is the Giver of gifts as well as the preferred Prize of all that He gives. Have you ever lost your balance?

Take a moment to remember just how far you've come with the Lord. If you feel you still have a long way to go, fear not, God uses ordinary people, just like you and me!

THE MOST
IMPORTANT PRAYER

After this manner therefore pray ye: Our Father which art in heaven, Hallowed be Thy name. Thy kingdom come. Thy will be done in earth, as it is in heaven. Give us this day our daily bread. And forgive us our debts, as we forgive our debtors. And lead us not into temptation, but deliver us from evil: For Thine is the kingdom, and the power, and the glory, for ever. Amen.
MATTHEW 9:13 (KJV)

The disciples asked the Lord to teach them how to pray. They had noticed that prayer was the helm that turned the ship toward the winds of destiny. When Jesus taught on prayer, He was teaching us how to steer the ship of life through the boisterous winds of adversity. If we can follow the "manner" of prayer, then we can follow the course of life.

In order to pray effectively, we must know the personage of God. Hence He said, *"Our Father."* This establishes the basis of the relationship that we have with God. He is more than just Creator. He is our Father. We can create something and not be related to it, but if we father it, a part of us will always be in the things we father. So I must know that I am related to God and not just created by Him. *"Which art in heaven"* addresses the fact that the God I am related to is the Ruler of the universe. He sits on the circle of the earth. The Bible teaches us that Heaven is God's throne. So when we say, "which art in heaven," we are proclaiming the absolute sovereignty of our Father. We say, in effect, "Not only are You my Father, but You also are uniquely qualified to answer my prayer. You are related to me and empowered to perform." This phrase points directly to God's position. Now knowing the person and the position of Him, let us praise Him.

"I am not ashamed to praise You as I know the extent of Your authority. I take this time to approach You correctly. *'Hallowed be Thy name.'* I almost forgot that just because You are my Father, my 'Abba,' that doesn't give me the right to show disrespect for Your position as Ruler in Heaven and earth. So 'hallowed be Thy name' reminds me that I must enter into Your gates with thanksgiving and into Your courts with praise." (See Psalm 100:4.) Praise will turn God's head. It will get His attention. I dare you to learn how to praise His name. When you praise His name, you are praising His character. He is "above board." He is holy!

PURPOSE POINT: When Jesus taught on prayer, He was teaching us how to steer the ship of life through the boisterous winds of adversity.

TRANSFORMATION MOMENT: The disciples had noticed that Jesus periodically would disappear from the crowd. He would steal away and fill His arms with the presence of His Father embracing Him so He could affect the people and us later. They asked Him to teach them too when they learned that the secret weapon of public success was just plain old prayer. It is not books, tapes, or videos; just groanings and moanings into the incense-filled altars of Heaven. In response to their request, Jesus taught His disciples to pray Matthew 6:9-13, so it must be a significant prayer. It should be one of our essential prayers.

Pray Matthew 6:9-13 out loud today. Focus on the first verses about who God is, Ruler in Heaven and on earth, Ruler of your life. Lift His name up today over every situation.

THE MOST IMPORTANT PRAYER (CONTINUED)

After this manner therefore pray ye: Our Father which art in heaven, Hallowed be Thy name. Thy kingdom come. Thy will be done in earth, as it is in heaven. Give us this day our daily bread. And forgive us our debts, as we forgive our debtors. And lead us not into temptation, but deliver us from evil: For Thine is the kingdom, and the power, and the glory, for ever. Amen.
MATTHEW 6:9-13 (KJV)

Today we will continue through this Matthew 6:9-13 prayer. It is the prayer we all need to steer the ships of our lives towards God's plans and purposes.

In the last entry we went through the first verse about who God is and lifting His name with praise. When praises go up, blessings come down. So here comes the downpour of power. *"Thy kingdom come"* releases the downpour of the power of God. Praise will cause the very power of God to come down in your life. But what good is power without purpose? Thus Jesus taught the disciples, *"Thy will be done in earth, as it is in heaven."* That is a step up from power to purpose. Now the purpose of God comes down to your life. Have you ever gone through a time that God began to show you His purpose in your life? You can't have success without purpose!

"*Give us this day our daily bread*" deals with the provisions of Heaven coming down. This is more than a prayer; it is a divine direction. After receiving the power in your life, you come to understand the purpose. Never fear; if you know your purpose, God will release the provisions. Then the provisions you couldn't reach at one stage in your life suddenly fall like an early morning drizzle at another stage in your life.

There's nothing like provisions to give you the grace to forgive. It is easier to forgive when you discover that your enemies didn't stop the blessing from coming down. Here Jesus teaches His disciples to pray for the penitence of a forgiving heart. "*Forgive us our debts, as we forgive our debtors.*" So penitence also is flowing down from the throne. Finally, Jesus taught us to seek deliverance from evil. Pray for the problems that still exist at every stage, and better still, at every success in life!

PURPOSE POINT: You can't have success without purpose! And never fear; if you know your purpose, God will release the provisions.

TRANSFORMATION MOMENT: If you were raised in church, you've probably prayed this Matthew 6:9-13 prayer hundreds of times. Little children learn this in Sunday school classes around the globe. Sometimes something becomes so familiar that we forget the meaning of the words behind it. I've taken the time to break apart the prayer Jesus taught His disciples because I want you to really understand how to pray. I want you to know what each word is communicating. Jesus based His ministry on the Father's voice. He didn't even start His ministry until the Father spoke over Him. Then He constantly broke free from the crowd to pray, to communicate with His Father.

This is how we ought to live our lives, constantly connected to God. Let this prayer go deep into your heart. Every word and phrase is a key to connection with your Father.

THE TURNING POINT

*...For thine is the kingdom, and the power,
and the glory, for ever. Amen.*
MATTHEW 6:13 KJV

Having briefly examined the progression of the believer through this precious prayer that Jesus taught His disciples, let us move on to the real point: the turning point. God wants you to receive all of the great successes and accolades that He promised in His Word, but having received them, you must go beyond them to enter a level of understanding. None of this success is as important or as valuable as you initially thought. At this stage of life you begin to reevaluate what you call success. God gets the glory when He can give you anything and you can turn from all He gave you and still say from your heart, "Lord, I've found nothing as dear to me as You. My greatest treasure is the assurance of Your divine presence on my life. I am giving it all to You. 'For Thine is the kingdom,'—yes, I know I just prayed it down, but here it is. I am giving it back to You. Wait a minute, Lord. I want to say something else. 'And the power.' You can have that too. Oh, and about all that glory I've been getting—it's Yours as well! What? You want to know how long? Forever and ever and ever. It is so! Amen!"

Every other aspect of creation that receives anything, gives it back to God. The gold cornfields of the Midwest give back seed after the heavens send down the rains. The singing sound of the busy bee fills the air with the testimony of the pollen it has taken from the lilac and the rose, but gives back in the sweetness of the honey packed tightly in the comb. All the lesser kingdoms give to a greater kingdom. The mineral kingdom gives strength to the vegetable kingdom. The vegetable kingdom is consumed by the animal kingdom. Everything reaches the point of return. How strong can an apple tree grow without reaching the point where it needs to give apples back to the ground it grew from?

PURPOSE POINT: God gets the glory when He can give you anything and you can turn from all He gave you and still say from your heart, "Lord, I've found nothing as dear to me as You."

TRANSFORMATION MOMENT: There must come in every person's life a turning point. Without it you can receive all of this power, purpose, provision, and penitence, overcome the problems, but still be burned out. If you fail to recognize and praise God, all your achievements will quickly lose their luster. There is no real joy outside of fellowship with Your Creator. Jesus cursed the fig tree because it had soaked up His water and flourished in His sun and yet, after all those blessings, had failed to reach the point of giving back one fig. We are created to receive and to give back heartfelt praises.

Pray this prayer one more time with me and truly give God all the glory, honor and praise for every accomplishment of your life (Matthew 6:9-13).

WALK OUT YOUR MIRACLE

*And they lifted up their voices and said,
"Jesus, Master, have mercy on us!"*
LUKE 17:13

No one can hear like the Lord does. He can hear the desperate cry of someone who has nothing left to lose. I can think of no better illustration than the ten lepers in the Bible (see Luke 17:11-19). These distraught, grossly afflicted men were entombed by the prison of their own limitations. No matter who they were before, now they were lepers, separated and cast out from friends and family. Like all alienated groups, their only refuge was in each other's company. Pain brings together strange bedfellows. Ten men huddled together on the side of the road heard that Jesus was passing by. The most frightening thing that could happen in any hurting person's life is for Jesus to just pass by. These men, however, seized the moment. They took a risk...they cried out to Him.

When the ten cried, He responded. He told them to go show themselves to the priest. Thus they walked toward a goal. Step by step they walked. I don't know which dusty step it was along the way that brought to them a cleansing of their leprous condition. Nevertheless, somewhere between Jesus' words and their going to the priest, they stepped into the greatest experience of their lives. Where there had been white, oozing, encrusted flesh, there was new skin as clear as a baby's. That is the wonderful thing about knowing Jesus— He takes away the old ugly scars of sin and leaves newness and fresh beginnings.

Ten men walked like hikers on the side of the road with nothing but a word from God. Beneath the clutter of their weary footsteps, God performed a miracle. Their healing meant much more than just a physical healing of leprosy. When Jesus healed them, He gave them back their dignity. He restored their potential to marry. He gave them back to their community. Thus success affects every area of life. Ten men giggling like children pulled at their clothes, gleefully showing each other their newly restored flesh. They had so much to do, so much to plan. The day seemed better and the sun much brighter. They probably floated over the road.

PURPOSE POINT: That is the wonderful thing about knowing Jesus—He takes away the old ugly scars of sin and leaves newness and fresh beginnings.

TRANSFORMATION MOMENT: Have you ever had a moment in your life that pushed you into a radical decision, where you cried out to Jesus like these desperate men? When they cried out, there were no sparks, no lightning, and no thunder, but the power of His words whisked them off into the realm of miracles. They were changed while in the process of obeying the command of a Savior whom they had called out to a few miles back on the dusty road where all miracles are walked out. Peeking beneath their clothes, checking spots that had once been afflicted, they laughed in the wind as the reality of their deliverance became even more real with every step they took.

Perhaps, as with most people, it is no one step that brings you to success, but a relentless plowing through of obstacles and insecurities that brings the result of prayers answered and miracles realized.

Day Eighty-Two

RETURN TO SENDER

*Every good gift and every perfect gift is from above,
and comes down from the Father of lights, with
whom there is no variation or shadow of turning.*
JAMES 1:17

Out of all ten lepers, one began to lag behind as his nine friends laughed and celebrated their victory. For him there was something missing. It wasn't that he lacked appreciation for his healing; it was just a nagging feeling that this great moment was somehow incomplete. He had been told to go show himself to the priest. But perhaps the real priest was not in front of him, but behind him, the Man on the road who spoke that word of healing.

Why was he so discontented with what the other men seemed to be satisfied? After all, had not the Man sent them on their way? He pivoted on his heels like a soldier who had heard a command. He had an impulse, a pulling toward something beyond personal allurement. He decided to return to the Sender. The Sender seemed to be satisfied, but it was the former leper who wanted something more. He traveled back to the Sender, Jesus, the Miracle Worker. When he came to Jesus, he fell down at His feet and worshiped Him. Then Jesus asked a question. It's seldom that Jesus, the omniscient

233

One, would ask anything—but this time He had a question. I shall never forget the pointedness of His question. He asked the one who returned, "Where are the nine?"

Ten men were healed, but to the one who returned Jesus added the privilege of being whole. Many will climb the corporate ladder. Some will claim the accolades of this world. But soon all will realize that success, even with all its glamour, cannot heal a parched soul that needs the refreshment of a change of peace. Nothing can bring wholeness like the presence of a God who lingers on the road where He first blessed you to see if there is anything in you that would return you from the temporal to embrace the eternal.

PURPOSE POINT: Ten men were healed, but to the one who returned Jesus added the privilege of being whole.

TRANSFORMATION MOMENT: Perhaps you are the one in ten who has the discernment to know that this blessing is nothing without the One who caused it all to happen. Most people are so concerned about their immediate needs that they fail to take the powerful experience that comes from a continued relationship with God! This is for the woman who goes back to the Sender of gifts with the power of praise. Remember, healing can be found anywhere, but wholeness is achieved only when you go back to the Sender with all of your heart and thank Him for the miracle of a second chance.

Don't be the other nine who forgot the Man who answered them in their most desperate moment. Don't settle for a miracle or a success story, daughter of God, receive the wholeness of life with Jesus.

THE JOY OF EVERY SEASON

TTo everything there is a season, a time for every
purpose under heaven: a time to be born, and a time
to die; a time to plant, and a time to pluck what is
planted; a time to kill, and a time to heal; a time to break
down, and a time to build up; a time to weep, and a
time to laugh; a time to mourn, and a time to dance.
ECCLESIASTES 3:1-4

Do you remember how in winter icicles hang from the roofs of old houses, pointing toward the ground like stalactites in a cave? As the cold blitz of winter was challenged by budding trees and warmer days, the icicles began to drip and diminish. Slowly the earth changed its clothes for a new season. I can plainly remember how as a child I felt the joys of each season. We packed away our sleds as spring came. We traded our coats for sweaters and then discarded them for just shirt sleeves as the sun liberated us from our wintry cocoons. In the silence of the night the sap that had hidden in the bottom of the trees moved upwards like a sluggish elevator making its ascent to the top. In the morning light buds turned to blossoms and by summer the blossoms showed their fruit.

Winter is just the prelude God plays to introduce the concerto of summer. In spite of its cold, frostbitten hand seizing our forest, lawns, and streams, its grip can still be broken through the patient perseverance of the season that is sensitive to timing and divine purpose.

There is nothing like a sense of time. It cannot be faked. It is like seeing a choir sway to the beat of a gospel ballad. Someone invariably will be moving spastically, trying desperately to simulate a sense of timing. Moving his feet with all the grace of the Tin Man in *The Wizard of Oz*, he can't quite learn what the body has to sense. The lack of timing is as detrimental as planting corn in the bitter winds of an Alaskan winter. There may be absolutely nothing wrong with the seed or the ground, just the time in which the farmer chose to expect the process to occur.

PURPOSE POINT: Winter is just the prelude God plays to introduce the concerto of summer.

TRANSFORMATION MOMENT: Everything has a season and a purpose (see Eccles. 3:1). You need to understand that God is just and that He appropriates opportunities to advance according to His purpose. I don't know whether this is true for everyone, but usually obscurity precedes notoriety. The first Psalm teaches that the blessed man meditates on the Word while he waits. It says that you bring forth fruit in your own season. It is good to recognize your season and prepare for it before it comes. But the fruit will not grow prior to its right season. Don't demand fruit when it is not in season. Even restaurant menus have a notation that says certain items can be served only when their fruit is in season.

Ask God to teach you His rhythm so you can move in sync with His seasons. Don't worry, dear daughter, you'll bear your fruit in the right time.

CONSULT THE ALMANAC OF GOD'S TIME AND PURPOSE

I would have lost heart, unless I had believed that I would see the goodness of the Lord in the land of the living. Wait on the Lord; be of good courage, and He shall strengthen your heart; wait, I say, on the Lord!
PSALM 27:13-14

Assuming that you now understand the necessity of small beginnings, and assuming that you realize whatever you have will not replace the One who gave it and that success only creates a platform for responsibility to be enlarged—then you can begin to ascertain where you are on the calendar, the divine almanac of God. Did you know that God has an almanac? Perhaps you do not know what an almanac is. My mother always consulted the almanac to determine the best time to plant the crop she intended to harvest. It is a calendar that presents the seasons and cycles of a year. You see, the principle of seed time and harvest will not override the understanding of time and purpose. God does everything according to His eternal almanac of time and purpose!

In autumn, you turn over the ground so last year's stalks and stems can become next year's harvest. Broken clods freshly turned, filled with crushed cornstalks and covered with manure, form the mulch you need to prepare the ground and replenish the starving soil after the previous yield. Like the ground that has given much and received little, you too need to be broken and turned over, allowed to rest for a time, and prepared for the next season of yield. If the ground produced without ever resting, it would soon be stripped of all the precious minerals it needs to be productive.

Ask God to give you the patience you need to become empowered to perform. You may feel like a child waiting in line at a carnival. There will always be times when other people receive their dues and you are forced to wait your turn. This is not injustice; it is order. There is nothing unjust about order. But after you have waited your turn and paid your dues, there comes a time when it is just your time!

PURPOSE POINT: God does everything according to His eternal almanac of time and purpose!

TRANSFORMATION MOMENT: Perhaps you have just completed a time of being turned over and undergoing manure-filled experiences. That period was just a prerequisite for a miracle! Thank God for the seasons of rest He gives to His children. When you've come through that season, your time for success will come too. When it does, don't forget to praise the God who gave you the wings to fly and the air to soar upon. Whatever season you're in, don't waste it. Just like the natural seasons, there is something important in each period of time. Each season is necessary to bring forth the fruit. Just as the Bible teaches us not to despise our small beginnings, we must not despise the timing of God.

Ask God to give you a deeper understanding of what season you're in. Ask Him to show you what's growing just beneath the surface. It's more glorious than you know!

WOMAN *Thou Art* BLESSED

FOR SUCH A TIME AS THIS

*For if you remain completely silent at this time,
relief and deliverance will arise for the Jews from
another place, but you and your father's house
will perish. Yet who knows whether you have
come to the kingdom for such a time as this?*
ESTHER 4:14

Mordecai taught Queen Esther an essential lesson when
he spoke those words. He wanted her to realize that
God had given her an opportunity to be a blessing. Now,
it wasn't given to her so she could brag about the nobility
of which she became a part. God isn't interested in human
grandeur. When He allows us to ascend into the clouds, it is
only so we can stop the rain with the enlightenment we gained
from the laborious progression of our own experiences.
Mordecai showed Esther that God had been grooming her all
her life for this moment. In spite of the tremendous challenge
set before her, she was the woman for the job. She was God's
choice, a handmaiden fitly chosen and wonderfully endowed
for the acquisition of a victorious report.

Mordecai's counsel prepared Esther's mind for the purpose God had from the beginning for elevating her position.
Counsel may prepare your mind, but only fervent prayer can

prepare your spirit for the vast undertakings that come with it being your time. No one counsel will prepare your heart like prayer.

Esther was a wise woman; she called a fast. Once Mordecai had exercised her mind through wise counsel, she called a time of fasting and prayer to prepare her spirit. She knew that prayer undergirds the spirit and keeps a person from sagging beneath the weight of opposition. Not only did she pray, but she also taught everyone under her authority to pray as well. I have learned that it is difficult to work with people who do not pray. Even our children pray. Now, I'm not suggesting that we are perfect. We don't pray because we are perfect—we pray because we are not! Prayer is a strong defense against satanic attack. If Esther had not prayed, she would have fallen prey to the cunning devices of Haman, her wicked enemy!

PURPOSE POINT: Counsel may prepare your mind, but only fervent prayer can prepare your spirit for the vast undertakings that come with it being your time.

TRANSFORMATION MOMENT: If you want to be part of God's great purposes on the earth, I admonish you to be a woman of fervent prayer. Esther was chosen by God for a significant mandate. God positioned her in a place of authority with great influence. She had the ear of the king, who had the power to save her people. If you want to be elevated to a position of influence, make sure you search your heart and motivations. If somewhere deep down, you're still looking for the affirmation of people, it won't go well for you. Esther did not take her position lightly. She knew she could only succeed in her mission if God backed her up, so she fervently sought Him.

Beloved, you have also have the ear of the King. He has placed you on the earth for such a time as this! Don't miss your time.

SOW IN TEARS, BUT REAP IN JOY

Those who sow in tears shall reap in joy. He who continually goes forth weeping, bearing seed for sowing, shall doubtless come again with rejoicing, bringing his sheaves with him.
PSALM 126:5-6

L
ike sands cascading down in an hourglass, time silently slips away, without the chance of retrieval, from almost everyone everyday. The misuse of anything as precious as time should be a crime. If someone steals your car, it would be an inconvenience but not a tragedy because you can easily acquire another. If someone snatches your wallet, it would be an annoyance but a few phone calls would salvage the majority of your concerns. But who can you call if you suffer the loss of time—and not just time, but *your time*? Who can afford to miss their time? I can't, can you?

The most frightening thing I can think of is the possibility of missing my time. Generally, somewhere on the other side of a tremendous test is the harvest of your dream. If you have planted the seeds of a promise and watered them thoroughly with the tears of struggle, then this is your time. Woe unto the person who has seeds without water. The tears of struggle become the irrigation of the Holy Spirit. It is through your own tear-filled struggles that God directs the waters of life to the field of your dreams.

On the other hand, you must know when you have shed enough tears. It is important that you don't get stuck in a state of lamentation. In short, don't overwater the promise! A certain amount of tears is necessary during the time of sowing. But when you have come into harvest, don't let the devil keep you weeping. Tears are for the sower, but joy is for the harvester. Harvest your field with joy. You've paid your dues and shed your tears—now reap your benefits. It's your turn. Reap in knee-slapping, teeth-baring, hand-clapping, foot-stomping joy!

PURPOSE POINT: Tears are for the sower, but joy is for the harvester. Harvest your field with joy.

TRANSFORMATION MOMENT: Greatness has a tremendous thirst. This thirst is quenched in the tear-stained struggle toward destiny. One thing I learned about life is neither fellowship nor friendship can lower the price of personal sacrifice. What I mean is, no one can water your dreams but you. No matter how many people hold your hand, you still must shed your own tears. Others can cry with you, but they can't cry for you! That's the bad news. The good news is there will be a harvest at the end of your tears! When you see it coming, trade your mourning for laughter.

If you are sowing in tears, take a moment to pause in God's presence. Ask Him if you've watered that ground enough. Only He knows the answer. Everyone goes through these seasons, but the important word is "through." There is another side to your sowing. There is a harvest of joy!

BE A PREPARED BELIEVER

Now it happened on the third day that Esther put on her royal robes and stood in the inner court of the king's palace, across from the king's house, while the king sat on his royal throne in the royal house, facing the entrance of the house. So it was, when the king saw Queen Esther standing in the court, that she found favor in his sight, and the king held out to Esther the golden scepter that was in his hand. Then Esther went near and touched the top of the scepter.

ESTHER 5:1-2

Esther's changing her apparel signifies our need to alter our circumstances to facilitate the success of the vision that is before us. Everything must be committed to the goal—body, soul, and spirit. When the king beheld a prepared person, he granted an expected end. He drew her into his presence because she had prepared herself for her time. Please hear me; there is a blessing on the horizon for the person of purpose. Only the prepared will be eligible to receive this endowment from the Lord, so be ready!

This is an exciting time for the prepared believer. I believe many are coming into "green light" times. You feel as though you have been waiting without seeing any results, almost like a car waiting at an intersection. Then the light suddenly changes from red to green and you are free to move. When God changes the light in your life from red to green, you can accomplish things that you tried to do at other times but could not perform. What an exciting time it is to suddenly find your engine kicking into gear and your turbines turning in harmonious production. Your tires screech from a dead stop to jet speed in seconds and bang! You are on the road again.

I believe with all my heart that soon people whom God had waiting their turn will burst to the forefront and pull into the fast lane. Trained by patience and humbled by personal challenges, they will usher in a new season in the cycle of the Kingdom. Are you a part of what God is doing, or are you still looking back at what God has done? I want to see you burn some spiritual rubber for Jesus!

PURPOSE POINT: I believe with all my heart that soon people whom God had waiting their turn will burst to the forefront and pull into the fast lane.

TRANSFORMATION MOMENT: I once met an evangelist at a retreat. He woke every morning while the rest of the ministers were still asleep and went jogging for hours in the early morning dew. When I awoke, he was coming down the hall with a flushed face and glistening with perspiration. He was smiling like he knew a secret. I asked him later, "Why don't you try to rest instead of racing around the grounds like you are preparing for a fight with Muhammad Ali?" He laughed, and I will never forget his answer. He said, "Every day I read for my mind. I pray for my spirit. And I run for my body." He explained, "If I touch all three areas, all parts of my being have been exercised to perform well."

To be a prepared believer is to actively get ready for what God wants to do in your life. Get ready, the light's about the change!

ANYWAY YOU BLESS ME, LORD

For the Lord God is a sun and shield; the Lord will give grace and glory; no good thing will He withhold from those who walk uprightly.

PSALM 84:11

There may be some degree of reservation in the mind of the thinking person. "What if I enter my season and experience the rich blessings God has been promising for a long time, and then the season ends? How can I stand to go back into seclusion and be content? Isn't it difficult, once a person has been a main player, to become subdued and lethargic after being exposed to the racing, titillating feeling of a green light time in life?" All of these are excellent questions, ones that must be addressed. After all, what good is having your season if over your head gather the gloomy clouds of warning that keep thundering a nagging threat in your ears? They threaten that all you are doing now will not last.

First, let me rebuke the spirit of fear. We need to declare God to this fear. We dare not fall in love with what God is doing, but we must always be in love with who God is.

God does not change. That's why we must set our affections on things that are eternal. His purpose doesn't change. His methods may change, but His ultimate purpose doesn't. People have a need to know what comes next. God doesn't always make us privy to such information, but He has promised that if we walk uprightly, He will not withhold any good thing from us (see Ps. 84:11). I therefore conclude that if God withheld it, then it was no longer working for my good. I am then ready for the next assignment—it will be good for me.

When I was a young man, there was an elderly lady in our church who used to sing a song that said something like this: "Anyway You bless me, Lord, I'll be satisfied." What a wonderful place to be in—a place where you can trust the God whom you have believed upon to operate for your ultimate good. He knows how much and how long to raise the crop in your field. There is a peace that Christians must have in order to enjoy life. You see, there always is an area where you can be fruitful; it simply may not be the same area all the time.

PURPOSE POINT: We dare not fall in love with what God is doing, but we must always be in love with who God is.

TRANSFORMATION MOMENT: The thing we must always remember is God can bless us in many different areas. Even while we were in the waiting periods of our lives, some other area was being blessed. There are really no "down" times in God. We only feel down when, like spoiled children, we demand that He continue to give us what He did at one stage without appreciating the fact that we are moving from one stage to another. It is what the Word calls going from faith to faith (see Rom. 1:17). God has put too much training into you to leave you without any area of productivity.

Can you sing that song too: "Anyway You bless me, Lord, I'll be satisfied"? Or are you losing sleep over what you don't have yet? Ask God to give you appreciation for the blessings you have right now.

WOMAN *Thou Art* BLESSED

COPY THE FARMERS AND DIVERSIFY YOUR HARVEST

*Preach the word; be prepared in season and
out of season; correct, rebuke and encourage—
with great patience and careful instruction.*
2 TIMOTHY 4:2 (NIV)

I believe one of Saul's greatest mistakes was to fall in love with the kingdom and not the King! He was so intimidated when God decided to move someone into his position that he tried to kill his successor. You would be surprised how many good people try to kill their successors. Mothers are jealous of their own daughters. Fathers belittle their own sons. If your time as a good boxer is up, then why can't you learn the art of being an excellent coach?

Speaking of coaches, the apostle Paul, who was an excellent minister of the gospel, began in the winter of his ministry to pour his knowledge into his successor. He wasn't jealous. He began the process of coaching the greatness that he recognized in the life of another man. Here he releases a concept that is very powerful. He counsels Timothy to develop the ability to be prepared in season and out of season. It seems almost conflicting to suggest that God wants us to be prepared in season as well as when our season seems to be receding. I could never quite understand this verse until another preacher began to share with me some farming techniques that I had not applied to this pursuit of excellence in ministry or in any other area.

The farmer who continuously produces crops can do so because he produces more than one type of crop. He has several different fields and he rotates a certain crop from one field to another. He plants corn in one field and it grows and produces ears of yellow corn on tall green stalks that sway in the wind and gleam in the sun. Eventually the corn goes out of season. The farmer takes the old stalks that turned brown and withered and plows them under. Now, a farmer always thinks in terms of tomorrow. He plows and fertilizes the field and allows it to rest from growing corn. Meanwhile in the other field the alfalfa is cut for the last crop of hay and it too is plowed. In the spring the farmer rotates his crops; the field that once grew corn now produces alfalfa, and the field that previously was planted in alfalfa now sprouts cornstalks. This coverall-clad soldier will always be productive because he understands the importance of being multifaceted.

PURPOSE POINT: This coverall-clad soldier will always be productive because he understands the importance of being multifaceted.

TRANSFORMATION MOMENT: Paul tells Timothy to be instant in season and out of season. He then tells him to be diverse. According to his instructions, we must reprove and rebuke. We also must be able to let things rest and encourage others. I believe many people lose their sense of self-worth because they fail to diversify themselves. Then, when the season of one gift is over, they are unprepared for any other area. If we listen carefully to the voice of God, we can be productive at every stage of life. It doesn't matter whether we are respected as players or as coaches. What matters is ultimately we contribute on some level to the game. We need to stay in the game. In short, diversity is a key to longevity.

How can you apply this to your own life and become a woman with diverse strengths? Invite the Holy Spirit to give you keys for diversity and readiness in and out of season.

IT'S YOUR TIME!

For as the rain comes down, and the snow from
heaven, and do not return there, but water the earth,
and make it bring forth and bud, that it may give seed
to the sower and bread to the eater, so shall My word
be that goes forth from My mouth; it shall not return
to Me void, but it shall accomplish what I please,
and it shall prosper in the thing for which I sent it.
ISAIAH 55:10-11

The Master has created a masterpiece in you. He has taken every struggle and test, every mishap and neglect, to cultivate in you the soil needed to make you reproductive. Contrary winds were sent to blow you away from people and cliques that would not create a climate conducive for what God wants to do in your life. In the light of His own divine "Sonshine," He has enlightened and established you. He is about to unveil a new realm of glory in your life.

What a celebration ought to be going on inside you at this moment. There ought to be a threefold celebration going on in your heart right now. First, you ought to look back over your times of obscurity, when He was plowing and fertilizing you, and thank God that you are still here to attest to His sustaining power. A lesser vessel would not have survived your testimony. Second, look around you at the blessings that you have right now. With a twinkle in your eye and a melody in your heart, thank God for what He is doing even at this moment. Your freshly cultivated ground is full of seeds and unborn potential. Who knows all that God has planted in you, beloved daughter. He has begun a work—a good work—in you. Celebrate that every time you wake up in the morning. Look over your straw-covered fields, fan back the birds of doubt and fear, and thank God. Breathe the fresh air into grateful lungs, being glad just to be here.

Third, you should celebrate what God is about to do in your life. Your heart ought to be thumping in your chest; your blood ought to be racing like a car engine about to peel rubber! You are about to step into the greatest harvest of your life. The enemy knows you are about to be harvested. That's why he fought you like he did. He realizes that this is your time. Don't you?

PURPOSE POINT: The Master has created a master-piece in you. He has taken every struggle and test, every mishap and neglect, to cultivate in you the soil needed to make you reproductive.

TRANSFORMATION MOMENT: A powerful prophetic move is about to explode over your life. Are you ready for the word of the Lord that was spoken over you to come to pass? Get ready! Hurry, get your mind ready, change your clothes! Put on your shouting shoes! When the news that's in your spirit gets in your mind, tears of joy will wet the runway for your takeoff. Don't ever read about anyone else and wish you were her. Don't ever wish you had lived at any other time. You were created for this moment—and this moment was created for you! Stop reading and look at the clock. Laugh to yourself and praise your God. Do you know what time it is daughter of God? *It's your time!*

ABOUT T.D. JAKES

T. D. Jakes is the #1 *New York Times* bestselling author of more than forty books and is the CEO of TDJ Enterprises, LLP. His television ministry program *The Potter's Touch* is watched by 3.3 million viewers every week. He has produced Grammy Award-winning music as well as hit films such as *Heaven Is For Real, Miracles from Heaven,* and *Jumping the Broom*. A master communicator, he hosts MegaFest, *Woman Thou Art Loosed,* and other conferences attended by tens of thousands.